The Lure and Lore of the
GOLDEN ISLES

The Lure and Lore of the
GOLDEN ISLES

The Magical Heritage
of Georgia's Outerbanks

DON W. FARRANT

RUTLEDGE HILL PRESS
Nashville, Tennessee

Published in Nashville, Tennessee, by Rutledge Hill Press, Inc., 211 Seventh Avenue North, Nashville, Tennessee 37219.

Typography by D&T/Bailey Typesetting, Inc., Nashville, Tennessee

Library of Congress Cataloging-in-Publication Data

Farrant, Don.
    The lure and lore of the Golden Isles : the magical heritage of Georgia's outerbanks / Don W. Farrant.
        p.   cm.
    Includes bibliographical references (p.   ) and index.
    ISBN 1-55853-262-5
    1. Golden Isles (Ga.)—History—Anecdotes.   I. Title.
F292.G58F37   1993
975.8'724—dc20   93-37413
                                                                      CIP

Printed in the United States of America
1 2 3 4 5 6 7 8 — 02 01 00 99 98 97

To Jean

*Who was always there
with loving encouragement.
She helped me along the way.*

CONTENTS

ACKNOWLEDGMENTS

I am indebted to these compatriots, who aided so much in the search for material. They all displayed patience with a persistent researcher:

Linda King, Director of the Coastal Georgia Historical Society, St. Simons Island; also, Linda's tireless assistants, Pat Morris and Lois Streett.

Librarians are always essential to a historical researcher, and I want to mention especially: Frances Kane and her assistants at the St. Simons Library; Diane Jackson, Dorothy Houseal, and Marcia Hodges at the Brunswick, Georgia Library; Del Presley at the Georgia Southern Library, Statesboro; John Christian at the Bryan Lang Library in Woodbine, Georgia; Barry Stokes at the Savannah Public Library; and all the fine personnel at the Florida Collections Section, Jacksonville Public Library.

Martha Teall, Jekyll Island Museum, for her special assistance while researching Jekyll Island lore.

Larry Latham, Mary Miller, Sam Cofer, Patricia Barefoot, Anita Timmons, and Mary McGarvey for special help in their particular areas of expertise.

Mildred Huie, Jasper Barnes, Tom Jenkins, Edward Ginn, and R. Edwin Green, all of St. Simons Island, for their cheerful help and encouragement.

The "out-of-town" gang, historians all, for their specialized background information: Gordon Smith, lawyer and researcher, Savannah; Robert Hurst, teacher and author, Waycross; Buddy Sullivan, author and editor, Darien; Dr. Stephen Wise, writer and Civil War historian, Beaufort, South Carolina; and Jack and Debi d'Antignac, Darien.

Finally, my wife, Jean, who helped type the manuscript and whose companionship and understanding made possible my labors.

—Don W. Farrant

INTRODUCTION

When, after several visits to the Georgia coast, my wife, Jean, and I decided to relocate to St. Simons Island, I looked around with wonder at its rich tapestry of history.

Having done some free-lance writing on historical subjects, I began submitting articles about the area to local and regional publications. I had little idea that the stories would achieve a certain measure of popularity. However, history buffs are congenial sorts and I made many friends and found myself gratified by the response.

It was a long time before I began to collect the pieces into book form. Others had suggested my doing so, but I was hesitant because the subjects I wrote about were so diverse in nature and lacked coherence as to subject matter. They fell into a time span of more than two hundred years, with nothing to connect them except that they were all "historical" pieces about the Georgia coast. Specifically, I concentrated on the chief barrier islands stretching from Savannah to the Florida border, and I included bits of nostalgia from such communities as Savannah, Midway, Brunswick, and St. Marys as well.

Finally, however, the book was a reality. While going over the final manuscripts, I found myself reflecting on something that has puzzled others: Just what is history? Is it "just the facts, ma'am" or do the best historians record their opinions? Without including a smattering of one's own whims, isn't one just a repeater of what others have distilled, a robot who grinds out bare (and perhaps boring) facts? Should historians set forth their own slants, along with the factual reporting?

I believe the reader likes for an author to interpret *lightly*, without heavy editorializing, to express whimsical, "peer-in-at-one-side" aspects of what happened while pulling it all into a form that's readable, dramatic, and possessed of a particular narrative thread.

This seems important: Does the historical article read like a real story? Does it have armchair appeal, so that people will enjoy sitting down and reading it? Does it have plenty of human interest? The right combination of these factors can make the dullest lineup of facts gripping, even unforgettable. It's that mixture of scholarly research and human triumphs (and failings) that so often produces sound, readable history. It is here that the writer makes history come alive.

In this volume I have tried to do just that. All through these pages you'll find the sidelights of people's thoughts and desires as they walked the beaches and wandered beneath the oaks in a land of legends, an area that has stirred the imaginations of explorers, artists, writers, and vacationers for many years.

If a dedicated woman, Lydia Parrish, had not spent years collecting and preserving the old slave songs, they would have been lost forever. If a slave, Liverpool Hazzard, had not lived to a ripe old age, there would have been no one who remembered how to make and race a dugout canoe in the style of the plantation era. If Christian Priber had never come to Georgia from Germany, we would not have the almost unbelievable tale of his life with the Cherokees and his attempts to found the Republic of Paradise where equality and harmony for all mortals was assured.

How could an eccentric millionaire build a large coastal home and then, jilted by his would-be bride, leave it and go into exile for more than thirty years? Who would believe that Georgia and Florida were actually on the verge of war, all because of a prize fight? It all happened, and we have the record here.

I hope you'll find *Lure and Lore* to be an easy-to-read collection of historical sketches, presented in a people-are-only-human sort of way and illuminated against the broader canvas of significant national happenings.

I have included a selective bibliography, one or two sources for each story. Personal interviews played a large role in the research. The nature of this presentation does not seem to demand an exhaustive bibliography.

I hope you agree that these accounts of the not-so-well-known characters of southeastern history, and some of the surprising events themselves, ought to be as much a part of our heritage as the great events of American history that are related in school textbooks.

COASTAL
CHARACTERS

*Dressed up for their wedding in 1903, here is Lydia
Stone and her first husband, George Stone.* [Courtesy
"Obediah's Okefenok" Historic Site, Waycross, Georgia]

ONE

LYDIA STONE
Queen of the Okefenokee

Lydia Stone didn't trust banks. She kept all her money at home (and folks said there was a lot of it). Maybe that explains why, when a stranger approached the house, she would appear on the front porch with a shotgun.

"That's far enough!" Lydia would command.

Just before the start of the Great Depression some bankers persuaded her that the only safe place for her money was a bank vault, so she made a sizable deposit. Came the bank holiday and it was generally thought that people would lose their hard-earned cash.

Not so Lydia Stone! It was said that she pounded on the windows of that bank, over and over, until someone let her in. She wouldn't leave until she got her money back.

Truth is stranger than fiction in the life of this big, tough, stern-voiced woman who prospered in lumber, cattle, and forest products in Brantley County, where she was known as the Queen of the Okefenokee.

Lydia was born in 1864 on Cowhouse Island at the edge of the great swamp. At an early age she learned the value of work and, lacking a formal education, soaked up plenty of practical knowledge. "Never went to school but six days in my life," she once announced, "but the man ain't living that can out-figger me."

She also said, "When I was a girl, my pappy gave me and

my sisters a cow and a sow apiece and told us if we would look after 'em we could make some money. Before the year was out I made a few dollars off'n mine and saved every penny of it."

A while later she picked up forty-five acres, dirt cheap. Whenever she was "money ahead" she would buy more acreage, sometimes acquiring cut-over land for less than a dollar an acre. She eventually owned around 30,000 acres.

Weighing almost 200 pounds, she packed plenty of power in her six-foot-plus frame. One early Brantley resident remembered, "I saw her take two railroad crossties and pick 'em up, one on top of the other."

Another time, Lydia came upon a workman who wanted to quit for the day because the woods were too wet and swampy to permit his mule and wagon to load the newly cut railroad ties. That didn't stop the Swamp Queen. "C'mon and help me," she said to the surprised workman as she marched into the woods (without the mule or wagon) and slogged back through the mud, hefting crossties on her shoulder. The man later reported it was one of his hardest days on the job—keeping up with "Miss Lydia."

One thing about the Swamp Queen: She was not afraid of work and her business enterprises made her a millionaire. She had a lot of men on her payroll, hauling timber and stumps and rounding up cattle, and she'd often get after "the boys" and tell 'em a few things. She was stronger than they were and could pick them right off the ground if she had a mind to. She could also cuss like a sailor.

She would ride around Cowhouse Island supervising the work, with her full-skirted dress hitched over the back of a horse or mule, wearing a white apron and a man's felt hat. She could round up her 600 head of cattle better than any cowboy and would thunder commands at her men like a drill sergeant.

Miss Lydia's business interests were varied. She sold

"Miss Lydia" poses with her second husband, J. Melton Crews, on their wedding day. [Courtesy "Obediah's Okefenok" Historic Site, Waycross, Georgia]

her cattle to markets in Waycross, her crossties to rail-road buyers in Jacksonville. Her pine stumps were valu-able for their rosin and pine oils, and these she could sell to the Hercules Corporation in Brunswick. She employed gum dippers to tap the trees and extract the gum so it could be sold to gum-dipping stills.

Most people thought she was tight with money because she was slow in paying her bills. She wanted to keep her hands on the money to use it up to the last minute. It was also said that she carried a gun in her little black pocket-book, which she was seldom seen without.

In 1903 Miss Lydia married George Stone. Apparently this was a happy union, despite the fact that he was domi-nated by his robust wife, tending to let her do the outdoor work while he became a sort of house husband. He died in 1926.

Then Cupid struck again. The Swamp Queen had her eye on a twenty-one-year-old employee who always plowed a straight furrow and cut his crossties to the proper length. He was J. Melton Crews, and even though Lydia, at age sixty-three, was forty-two years his senior, they were married in 1927. She called him "Doll Baby" and made him wear his hair long and grow a beard so he would look older.

Later Doll Baby was involved in a shooting incident and accused of murder. While he was doing time in At-lanta, Lydia visited him often and expended every effort to gain his release, which she finally achieved through a well-placed bribe—or so folks said.

When Miss Lydia died in 1938 at the age of seventy-three, she left Doll Baby a generous fortune. Her head-stone at High Bluff Cemetery rises over all the others, symbolic perhaps of one who was commanding in her lifetime.

Miss Lydia's secret of success was simple enough: just stick to business. "I always said I could make five dollars out of every one dollar I could get my hands on," she claimed. "I believe anybody can if they're careful and not afraid to work."

TWO

McEvers Brown
Oddball Millionaire

The list of characters who left an imprint on the Golden Isles would not be complete without the name of McEvers Bayard Brown.

An eccentric millionaire, he was one of the original members of the Jekyll Island Club and the first to build a house there. But, alas, when he was jilted by his bride-to-be, he left his honeymoon home forever, fled to England, and lived in solitary seclusion on a yacht for thirty-six years.

Few life stories have such bizarre dimensions. Brown was born "in the money" in New York in 1853 and, as a young man, was active in the social swirl, being described as good-looking and elegantly dressed. Thus he was eligible for the Jekyll Island Club and the other millionaires welcomed him as a member in 1886.

Apparently the well-heeled bachelor liked Jekyll, although he spent little time there. He ordered construction of a grand house, which was completed in 1888. His "cottage" overlooked the marshes close to what is now the south end of the Jekyll airstrip. Part of the chimney foundation can still be seen, and a historical marker stands at the spot.

The true story may never be known, but rumor has it that Brown built the place expecting his beloved to join him there. When she didn't, the broken engagement drove him into exile. It may have also twisted something in his mind. In 1890 he sailed to England and moored his 63-ton yacht near a sleepy village on the Essex coast. Here he felt insulated against the sorrows and memories of his native land, and he soon replaced his floating home with a more luxurious yacht, a 1,000-tonner originally built for the Prince of Wales.

Now comes one of the most perplexing chapters in a mysterious life: Brown lived aboard the ship in seagoing splendor but his yacht never went anywhere. Even more astounding, he retained a crew of eighteen for many years and kept his boilers stoked and ready to sail at a moment's notice. The men, in fact, grew old and gray in his service and some even died while awaiting orders to put to sea.

What did Brown do all this time? Said to be a sharp businessman, he dealt in investments and real estate speculation, making occasional trips to London. He had a loyal private secretary for thirty-four years, a Major Sturdee, but neither he nor any of Brown's employees were permitted to sleep aboard the yacht.

Many stories were told about the oddball American. He refused to allow visitors aboard and would occasionally toss lumps of coal at sightseers who got too close. Anyone who mentioned America to him would be met with a stern, tight-lipped silence. There were times when he suspected the coal in his bunkers contained dynamite, so he'd have it thrown overboard. Again and again he greeted people with the question, "Any claims or penalties?" No one ever knew what he meant.

During World War I, British authorities required Brown to vacate his moorings, but he simply sailed upriver and put his ship into a drydock for much-needed repairs. After the war he remained on the yacht, living in the plainest fashion and getting more and more inactive until his death in 1926 at age seventy-three.

At the news of his passing there was sorrow in the

English countryside. He had become something of a legend and it came out that he had given more than $250,000 to the Essex communities for parks, schools, hospitals, and charities. At his death, his income was said to be close to $1 million a year.

Brown's body was returned to New York where he was buried, according to his wishes, next to his father. The story goes that one of the mementos found among his belongings was the charred remains of a photo of a young woman.

Although Brown never lived in his Jekyll cottage and probably never saw the finished structure, he retained his membership in the Jekyll Island Club for years and was generous in granting use of the house as living quarters for club employees. Also, he contributed substantially to the liquidation of the club's debt.

THREE

CHRISTIAN PRIBER

Prime Minister of Paradise

People were drawn to the fellow, for he had a way about him. He had a courtly bearing, highly persuasive powers, and fluency in many languages.

To the Cherokee Indians he became a messiah, a sort of cult leader, and they liked his concept of the ideal community. It would be named the Republic of Paradise, and he would be its prime minister.

When he set up his wilderness kingdom among the Indians way back in the 1700s, he nearly made it work. Then it came crashing down around him.

Christian Gottlieb Priber was born in the German electorate of Saxony in 1697. A scholar and a utopian philosopher, he married and raised five children before loftier notions than mundane family matters caused him to part company with his German family around 1731.

When he decided America was the place to put his startling doctrines to work, Priber booked passage to Charleston, arriving sometime in the early 1730s. But he didn't intend to stay. In 1735 he advertised that he was divesting himself of all worldly goods. His possessions sold quickly, thanks to low "close-out" prices, and then the man seemed to vanish from the face of the earth.

Priber somehow made his way 500 miles across the

Appalachian Mountains carrying paper, ink, and a trunkful of books. In a short time rumors began drifting to the coast about a strange man, educated and speaking many languages, who lived with the Indians at Tellico, chief village of the Cherokees in East Tennessee. He had personal magnetism, claimed the traders and scouts who had met him, and was trying to form an unusual society that was not like any other.

Priber's society would be different all right. Years before Thomas Jefferson wrote the Declaration of Independence, he was maintaining that all men are born free and equal and would be welcome in his Republic of Paradise, of which he was the prime minister.

He visualized a utopia, which would be a haven for debtors, felons, servants, and slaves, where property would be owned in common and "all crimes tolerated except murder and idleness." The best government, in his opinion, was one that governs least and so the only laws of Paradise would be those needed to implement the laws of nature. Citizens would be free to change marriage partners as often as desired.

What alarmed the English, however, was that this puppet monarch was stirring up the Indians, telling them they had been tricked out of their lands and they should make no further concessions to British authorities. On top of that, he was also making friendly overtures to the French, bitter enemies of the English. Therefore, Gen. James Oglethorpe, at Fort Frederica, decided something had to be done.

In 1743 Priber was traveling in what is now Alabama, in an effort to unite the southern Indians in one huge league. Captured by a force of Oglethorpe's men, he was taken to Frederica and jailed. Priber was doomed to spend the rest of his days as a captive in the barracks, with a sentry constantly pacing outside his door. Meanwhile, back at Tellico his Indian wife waited for him in vain, and without his leadership his republic collapsed.

Priber was a model prisoner. Such was his personality

that he never displayed anger or resentment, and visitors marveled at his cheerfulness in the face of adversity.

"My mind soars above misfortune," he said. "I can forgive and pray for those who injure me."

The philosopher was allowed to write his memoirs while in prison, but when he died in confinement (date unknown), his manuscript disappeared mysteriously. No trace of it has ever been found.

After his death, fearful stories began to circulate around the town of Frederica. A whitish, misty apparition had been seen, wandering around and haunting the place. Was Priber looking for his lost memoirs?

Or was the ghostly figure just searching for someone to listen to his tales of the ideal community, this Republic of Paradise?

FOUR

SIDNEY LANIER

Poet of the Marshes

Starving artists of the world, take heart from
the life of Sidney Lanier! Viewing the ups and downs he
went through, one marvels that he sustained himself, his
family, and his art as well as he did. There's no doubt
about it, life was hard for the poet who immortalized the
marshes of Glynn and the Florida mockingbird.

Sidney, a Macon native, was born in 1842. An artistic
temperament showed up early, for he loved classical music and literature and seems to have acquired the de-
meanor and habits of a southern gentleman. He dabbled
in poetry and became an accomplished flute player. After
graduation from Oglethorpe University in 1860, Sidney
mingled in the best circles, living the life of a popular,
urbane man about town.

Then along came the Civil War. In 1861 he enlisted in the
Second Georgia, Macon Volunteers, the first unit to leave
the state for Virginia. After a year of service he was transferred to Petersburg, then to blockade-running duty. After
a few months of exciting chases his vessel was captured by
a Federal patrol boat and he was sent to one of the worst
Union prison camps.

The young man had never been overly robust and in
prison he was quartered in a tent, given only meager ra-

tions, and subjected to crowded, unsanitary conditions. He contracted severe fevers and, finally, tuberculosis. By the time he was discharged at the war's end his health was permanently affected. Later, thinking back to the glory days of war service, he said, "What fools we were!"

A civilian once more, Sidney spent his time teaching and clerking, while writing poetry on the side. Maintaining his love for music, he also perfected his flute playing while suffering many coughing spells and an occasional lung hemorrhage. In 1867 he married Mary Day, a Macon girl, and this was destined to be a happy union.

Next came a period of striving to maintain financial stability while coping with serious health problems. His expertise with the flute got him a symphony orchestra job in Baltimore at sixty dollars a month, but this required traveling, which was difficult for his family and hard on his health.

In 1874 Mary was staying with relatives in Brunswick and Sidney came down for a visit. He enjoyed the seacoast climate and took daily carriage rides, usually to a restful place where he could scan the broad vista of the marshes. This was good therapy and for a while his health seemed to improve. Sometimes he would sit for hours, making notes and taking in the beauty of the scene before him. The result was one of the greatest poems to emanate from the Southland, "The Marshes of Glynn." A tree at this spot, alongside present-day Highway 17, was known as Lanier's Oak and a historical marker has been placed there.

The poem describes a day on the marshes. Before noon the poet walks into a forest of live oaks, which are covered with festoons of Spanish moss. As the sun begins to sink, he passes to the sand beach where he looks over the tall marsh-grass to the sea and watches the tide come in. He is filled with a sustaining confidence in God:

By so many roots as the marsh-grass sends in the sod I will heartily lay me a-hold on the greatness of God. O, like to the greatness of God is the greatness within the range of the marshes, the liberal marshes of Glynn.

As the 1870s wore on, there was constant struggle for Sidney to provide for his family and to cope with his worsening tuberculosis. He was nearly destitute when a commercial opportunity came his way. The Atlantic Coast Railway wanted a guidebook promoting Florida to the tourists. Although his artistic nature rebelled at such work, he took the job (for the money) and produced what later became a collector's item: "Florida—Its Scenery, Climate and History."

The poet rested in Florida for a while after the guidebook was finished and he should have stayed longer, for the warm sunshine soothed his illness. But money again ran short, and he made a trip to New York in the spring of 1881. Later that year, in a seriously weakened condition, he moved again, this time to Lynn, North Carolina. Sidney died on September 7, 1881, at the age of thirty-nine.

But the artist for whom various landmarks are named, including the Lanier Bridge in Brunswick, left a rich heritage in his verses, and more than one of his works was influenced by his beloved marshes. . . . Included in the list are "Sunrise," "Sunset," "Marsh Hymns—Between Dawn and Sunrise," and "Individuality."

FIVE

NEPTUNE SMALL

The Slave Who Gave His All

In Neptune Park on St. Simons Island a serene landscape of nature walks is set off by giant oaks whiskered with Spanish moss.

One might think the area honors Neptune, the classical god of the sea, but instead, the park is dedicated to the memory of a loyal slave named Neptune Small.

Owned by the planter Thomas Butler King, he was not assigned to the cotton fields but to look after the three sons of the family, especially Henry Lord Page King. Neptune was devoted to "Mas' Lord," whom he had tended since boyhood, waiting on him and cooking his meals in the style of the old South.

In 1862 all the King sons went off to fight for the Confederacy. Neptune accompanied Capt. Lord King as his bodyservant. The two were at Fredericksburg when Southern forces massed to repel a Union advance.

One night there was such a movement of troops and artillery that Neptune was sure there would be a major battle the next day. As he cooked supper near the Confederate lines, he noticed Lord was staring into the fire with a faraway look in his eyes.

"Supper ready, young master," said the slave.

Before turning to the simple repast, King said, "A lot of good men will eat their last supper tonight."

Neptune Small was a slave of the Thomas Butler King family. Here is pictured in later life, around 1900.
[Courtesy Coastal Georgia Historical Society]

The next morning Neptune watched as the captain went off to join his unit. All day he heard the sounds of battle and that night he cooked as usual, as he waited for his master to return. Several times he stirred the fire to keep the food warm, but no Mas' Lord. Still hearing the cannon and muskets, he said to himself, "Day ain't through yet."

Neptune didn't realize this was the bitterest day of fighting at the Battle of Fredericksburg, December 13, 1862.

After dark, the servant went out to the battlefield and began searching among the bodies. Later he recalled there were "dead mans everywhere but none look like Mas' Lord."

Finally he found his master, lying face down. Someone had stolen one of his boots, leaving the other because it was so bloody. Neptune turned him over so he could see his face. "Mas' Lord, supper is ready. I been waitin' for you. Is you hurt bad?"

There was no answer. Picking up Lord's body, Neptune carried it from the field. Then began an incredible display of determination as the servant transported the body hundreds of miles back home to Georgia.

Neptune first went to Richmond, accompanying a pine box into which Confederate medical officers had placed his master's body (probably after a temporary embalming job). In Richmond Neptune bought the best coffin he could find and continued his long journey south.

It is unclear what methods of transportation he used but he somehow struggled through the chill of winter along rugged roads and trails and across several rivers and marshes. Neptune arranged for the body to be interred in Savannah, but later, members of the King family had it moved. The young soldier was laid to rest in the family plot at Christ Church on St. Simons.

Such was Neptune's dedication to the family that he then returned to the Virginia battlefields to be with the youngest son, R. Cuyler King. The two were together until the end of the war.

Reconstruction days were hard on all the coastal plantations. The Kings were forced to vacate and for a time their fields were overgrown with weeds. Finally, when they returned, Neptune came with them. He adapted well to the life of a free man, doing various maintenance jobs for the Kings and helping them rebuild the home, Retreat, into something of its former prominence. He was given a tract of land to build a small house on what is now Neptune Park near the pier at St. Simons Island.

One of Neptune's tasks was cemetery upkeep. Here,

once again, he demonstrated his loyalty and devotion. Tenderly, he would clean leaves and rubbish from Lord King's grave, caring for it as he had cared for his young master in life. He continued to do this until he was white-haired, stooped, and full of years. Neptune Small passed away at St. Simons on August 10, 1907, at the age of seventy-five. His grave lies in a small cemetery reserved for domestic servants near the site of the old King plantation house.

Today golfers who play the lush Sea Island course give hardly a passing glance at the little graveyard beside the fairway. How can they know the tremendous human drama represented by the headstone marked "Neptune Small: 1831–1907"?

On February 18, 1994, a commemorative plaque was dedicated at Neptune Park near the pier at St. Simons Island. At the same time, a live oak was planted in memory of the old former slave. Taking part in the dedication ceremony were two of Small's great-grandsons, Jasper Barnes of St. Simons, and William Barnes of Frederick, Maryland. The plaque, containing a brief history of Neptune's life, reads as follows:

NEPTUNE SMALL

For generations residents and visitors alike have enjoyed Neptune Park, named for Neptune Small, a faithful servant of the Thomas Butler King family at Retreat Plantation, now home of the Sea Island Golf Club. Born into slavery in 1831, Neptune accompanied one of the King sons, Henry Lord Page King, as manservant when he enlisted in the Confederate Army. During the Battle of Fredericksburg in 1862, Captain King volunteered for a dangerous mission and was killed. When night fell, Neptune retrieved King's body and brought it home for burial in the family burial ground at Christ Church, Frederica, St. Simons. Although he could have chosen to remain at home, Neptune returned to war as manservant to the youngest King son, R. Cuyler King. After the war the King family gave this portion of Retreat Plantation to Neptune who, as a freedman, had chosen "Small" as his last name for this slight stature. Neptune died in 1907 and is buried in the Retreat burial ground. This marker and live oak tree are given and dedicated by Sea Island Company to his memory.

SIX

WILLIAM CONE

Frontier Fighter

Early Georgia history had its share of rip-roaring, devil-may-care adventurers. Of this breed, it's hard to top Capt. William Cone, soldier, Indian fighter, and popular citizen of Camden County.

As with many citizens of the eighteenth century, Cone's life was a reflection of the struggles and privations of the times. Born in North Carolina in 1777, the son of an American Revolutionary War officer, he left the family homestead at an early age for Bulloch County, Georgia, and from there moved to Camden County sometime around 1806.

Plenty of action abounded on the frontier in those days. Indians would go on the warpath, and young Cone, who was tough of body and a fine woodsman, would join the settlers in forays against them. As a scout in the War of 1812 he helped safeguard American troops against the British.

Cone, however, wasn't too busy to get married. In 1812 he took Miss Sarah Haddock as his bride and to this union were born five children.

In 1815 the British captured the town of St. Marys. After the occupation came one of the most remarkable episodes in the annals of American warfare when the

Redcoats piled into twenty-three barges and headed up the St. Marys River, their mission being to burn some valuable sawmills. But the British were ambushed by a force of twenty-eight men under the command of Captain Cone. These riflemen, it seems, were confronted with a bunch of "sitting ducks" and made the most of their opportunities.

Firing at the barges from shore, the Americans were able to inflict heavy casualties without being seen. Hiding behind palmettos, they kept up a running fire all along the river until the British were forced to retreat to St. Marys. The deadly hail of bullets took 180 British lives, wounding a similar number. There is no record of any casualties on the other side.

After the war Cone developed a new talent: "collecting" Indian horses. With a small band of followers, he would sneak across the Florida border, steal ponies and cattle, and drive them back to Georgia. Soon he had a reputation for daring and cunning, and the Indians held him in awe, finding him impossible to capture.

However, Cone's luck eventually ran out. Returning from a successful trip, his party was overtaken and in the scuffle he was wounded in the neck. He fell from his horse and was taken prisoner.

The Indians were exultant at having captured the Big Captain, as they called him. They trussed him up and started home to Florida, probably intending to torture him.

But the wily Cone outwitted them again. As they camped one night, he managed to slip out of his bonds and remove the bullets from the Indians' guns. Knowing he could not get far in his weakened condition, he decided not to flee but to resort to strategy. He sat on a nearby log and waited.

At dawn, when his captors discovered him sitting on the log, one of them fired a gun at him. Cone pretended to catch the bullet in his hand. He showed it to the Indians, then put it in his pocket. Others shot at him with the same results and finally, convinced that the man was supernatural, the Indians fled in terror, leaving all the horses. Cone mounted one, and began moving slowly because of his neck wound. He managed to herd the rest of the horses and make his way home to Camden.

Although Cone was not an educated man, he was certainly a patriot, always dedicated to serving his country in a vigorous and honorable way. Later in life he was a member of the state legislature, being especially noted for loquaciousness and force of character.

This rough-hewn frontier fighter died in Florida in 1857, at age eighty.

SEVEN

LIVERPOOL HAZZARD

A Slave Who Remembered

No one knows why he named himself Liverpool. No one knows whether he actually lived to age 110. One thing is sure: Liverpool Hazzard, born in slavery, remembered the events, the people, the plantations in their glory days.

Yes, there are mysteries about Liverpool, but they only add to his mystique. His life spanned some of the mighty rumblings of American history: slavery, the Civil War, Reconstruction, a world war, and the twentieth century with its social and technological upheavals. Liverpool knew it all and shared his knowledge, to the entertainment and enlightenment of others.

Historian Margaret Davis Cate says he was born in 1828, but that was a time when birth records were scarce, so nobody knows for sure. Anyway, he was a Butler slave and proud of it. Among the holdings of Pierce Mease Butler was a rice plantation on Butler Island in the delta of the Altamaha River and there, in antebellum days, the young man spent his time.

Assuming the year of his birth is correct, he was a lad of eleven when Fanny Kemble, wife of Pierce Butler, visited Butler Island. Although she only stayed a few months, Liverpool, in his old age, would say he "remembered his first missus."

Liverpool and his ox cart.

Fanny Kemble was a talented English actress and writer who married Butler, then came down from Philadelphia to inspect the family holdings. She was aghast at the treatment of slaves and wrote gruesome details in her journal, later published during the Civil War as *Journal of a Residence on a Georgia Plantation.*

The book was something of a sensation in England and is said to have been a strong influence in the British decision not to grant a substantial loan to the Confederacy.

His manner and intelligence made Liverpool stand out and his master selected him as a household servant. He also performed as an oarsman. However, during the Civil War (when in his thirties), he was the cook for a company of Southern soldiers commanded by Capt. William Miles Hazzard, working out of Camp Walker on the mainland in

Glynn County. This explains where the name *Hazzard* came from; the captain had been the slave's last master, so he took his name.

In later years, Liverpool fondly remembered when he was sent into a swamp with a group of Confederate soldiers to hide some horses so that Yankees in the area would not find them. The men had to hold their hands over the mouths of the horses so they would not neigh and be detected. It worked, and Liverpool always chuckled about this, for it gave him a sense of pride to have been a part of the successful scheme. After the war, Liverpool was employed by the Butler plantation as a handyman and he also "sat in" at the oars of plantation dugouts. It was in 1867 that he rowed his desperately ill former master, Pierce Butler, to the doctor in Darien. After Butler's death, he worked for Butler's daughter, Frances Butler Leigh, who continued to operate the plantation for several years. Her book, *Ten Years on a Georgia Plantation*, gives a vivid picture of life during Reconstruction.

Living well into the twentieth century, Liverpool claimed a little cabin in Darien as home, and a granddaughter who lived nearby cooked for him and took care of his needs. He had a unique way of getting around: "There's Liverpool and his ox cart!" folks would say. Indeed, this was a familiar sight, and even though it took hours to get somewhere due to the slowness of the beast, he didn't seem to mind. Liverpool and the ox had been partners a long time and seemed to understand each other.

In the 1920s and 1930s, he became something of a tourist attraction. When he was (supposedly) 107 years old, an enterprising fellow put a fence around his cabin and charged admission to see him. Liverpool allowed this, with one hitch: None of his friends should have to pay. His promoter painted "107" on the fence in huge letters. Even though he lived for three years after that, the sign was never changed.

In 1929, Liverpool helped design and build a couple of dugout canoes at Darien. They were cut from immense

Liverpool Hazzard: Born, St. Simon's, 1828—Died, Darien, 1938. [Courtesy Sea Island Company]

cypress logs with the idea of giving the public a look at what plantation racing canoes were like and perhaps to revive the sport. One of those involved in the project was Howard Coffin, developer of Sea Island and the Cloister Hotel. The boats were exact replicas of the old dugouts and attracted plenty of publicity, but there was insufficient interest for a rebirth of old plantation style rowing.

While he was advising the boat builders, Liverpool was interviewed by the press. He related that watermen on the Butler plantation got special treatment but had to observe strict training rules. "The marster wouldn't let us do physical labor for four months before a race," he claimed, "and he would lock us up if we did. We would just eat and practice to make our muscles strong!"

He continued, "The marster would bet $500 on us every time, and when we won there was sure some celebratin'. We'd all stay up all night and all the others would make a fuss over us."

Before he passed away in 1938 at age 110 (some said he was only 85), he had a lot of friends who helped care for him, as well as Lady Alice Butler. She was Frances Leigh's daughter, who had married Sir Richard Pierce Butler, a distant relative. For a long time she kept in touch with all the old Butler plantation blacks and loved to throw big parties for them and their descendants on special occasions.

EIGHT

EUGENE O'NEILL

He Thought He'd Never Leave

Near the Cloister Hotel on Georgia's Sea Island stands the Eugene O'Neill Oak, a landmark donated by Connecticut College in New London. The tree is a tribute to America's greatest playwright, who lived on Sea Island from 1931 to 1936.

O'Neill had some rough times in his early life and it might have contributed to his later temperament and moods. His father was a traveling actor and, as a boy, he was shuttled from hotel to hotel. The family's only real home, which Eugene would remember fondly later in life, was a summer place at New London, Connecticut.

He had already had one unsuccessful marriage when, at the age of twenty-six, he decided to become a playwright. At first his efforts were mediocre, but he began to catch on with the public and was soon penning a series of successes, including *Anna Christie, The Emperor Jones,* and *Desire Under the Elms.* His most successful play was *Strange Interlude* (1928) and royalties from this production made him wealthy.

In 1931 O'Neill needed a rest after completing *Mourning Becomes Electra,* a trilogy, in New York. He and his third wife, Carlotta, stayed at the Cloister for a month. They liked it so well they decided to build a house on Sea Island.

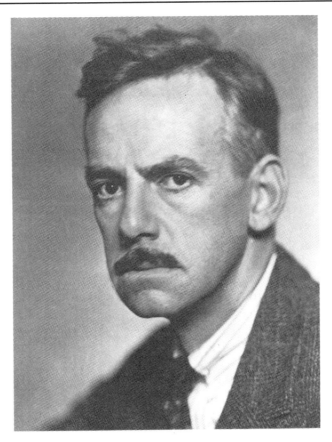

Eugene O'Neill thought he never would leave his home on Sea Island, but he did— in 1936. He is considered America's greatest playwright.

O'Neill was extravagant, engaging a noted architect and erecting a stately seaside home that was a blend of early Majorcan peasant and sixteenth-century monastery styles. The couple whimsically dubbed it Casa Genotta, a sort of Italian-ish combination of their names, Gene and Carlotta. They reportedly spent $100,000 on it—a substantial amount at the time—and they bought extra parcels of land around the house for privacy. Above the dining room

O'Neill set up a studio where he wrote, standing up, at a high captain's desk.

While at Sea Island, O'Neill made notes for his monumental *Long Day's Journey into Night*, which was not staged until 1956, after his death. In 1932, while immersed in the philosophical drama *Days Without End*, he awoke one morning with an idea for a comedy based on his youth in New London. Vigorously, he began to sketch it out.

The result was *Ah Wilderness*, completed in a month. This was well received and O'Neill said it "showed the way I would have liked *my* boyhood to have been." Critics now said he had matured and praised him for turning painful childhood memories into a comedy with a life of its own.

Alfred ("Bill") Jones, one of the founders and original executives of Sea Island, said that O'Neill was the only authentic genius he had ever known. Genius he was, but there is evidence that his life was often in turmoil. He once noted, "Half of me is playing the fiddle while Rome burns, and the other half is going up in the conflagration!"

At his island home the playwright was visited by luminaries from the literary and theatrical worlds, including Sherwood Anderson, Somerset Maugham, Lillian Gish, and Bennett Cerf. The influx of visitors caused Carlotta to become strangely protective. She acted more and more as a gatekeeper, becoming less patient with the friends she did not favor and finding ways to exclude them. As a result, O'Neill must have gained time for his work, but he probably spent too many hours alone, working in solitude.

When the weather was right, however, the playwright enjoyed his recreation. He swam daily in the ocean, causing Carlotta to worry for his safety when he went out too far. He tried his hand at surf fishing, and Bill Jones remembered that he had a favorite fishing spot on the Hampton River.

The O'Neills left their island home in 1936, and one of

the reasons was said to be the hot Georgia sun. In the fall of that year he was awarded the Nobel Prize for literature. In his career, he also won four Pulitzer Prizes and other awards.

As time went on there were many disappointments for Eugene O'Neill. He could not match his earlier successes and, during the 1940s, he was plagued with an increasing tremor in his hands, among other maladies. When he realized he could not continue his writing, he became moody and irritable.

Gene and Carlotta lived for a time in California, then moved to New York and later to Massachusetts. Their marriage, though stormy, somehow survived. Finally, sick, bitter, and disillusioned, O'Neill died in a Boston hotel in 1953 at the age of sixty-five. Carlotta lived for several more years, then passed away in 1970 at a nursing home in New Jersey.

NINE

JOHN H. DEVEAUX

A Life of Service and Achievement

He stepped forward and did his duty, unflinchingly, in the face of a dreadful disease. He was an early example of a black man who was a leading citizen—and a hero too.

John H. Deveaux was born in Savannah in 1848. Although he was in the category of "free black," his opportunities were little better than those of slaves. Forbidden by the Black Codes to learn to read or write, he somehow secured a solid education, probably through a family friend who ran an informal school in her home. Later, he was lucky enough to be chosen by a prominent Savannah doctor as his ward.

During the Civil War, Deveaux, at age sixteen, became a Confederate mess boy, or steward. In 1864 he joined a group of rebel raiders in an attack on the Federal gunboat *Water Witch*, moored in Ossabaw Sound, just south of Savannah. When the warship was captured, it was a boost for the Southern cause. In this action the commander of the raiding party, Lt. Thomas Pelot, was killed. Deveaux cared for the officer's body until he could return it to the family. In later years he laid a wreath on Pelot's grave each year on the anniversary of his death.

Colonel John Deveaux was said to be completely devoid of selfishness and rarely spoke ill of anyone. A career servant in the U.S. Customs Service, he was a hero of the yellow fever epidemic in Brunswick in 1893.

In 1870 Deveaux, at age twenty-two, secured an appointment as a clerk of the Savannah Customs Office, the start of a career that would span thirty-nine years. Holding increasingly important posts in the U.S. Customs, Deveaux became known for his integrity and won the respect of fellow townspeople, both white and black.

In 1889, President Benjamin Harrison appointed Deveaux collector of customs at Brunswick. He had been the unanimous choice of black Republicans but there was immediate opposition from some local groups and the white press. A delegation went to Washington to protest but failed to dislodge Deveaux. He gave a flawless performance in his new capacity.

When a yellow fever epidemic broke out in Brunswick in 1893, Deveaux won praise for sticking to his job. He kept the customs office open and, even though some of his clerks were stricken, almost single-handedly attended to the entering and clearing of port vessels. When he was assigned to distribute $40,000 in relief money to sufferers, he did it to the satisfaction of all.

Actually, Deveaux was merely repeating what he had

done at Savannah during the yellow fever epidemic of 1876. On that occasion one of his fellow clerks died and others came down with the disease, including the collector, leaving him the only official on duty. Before the raging plague was over, Deveaux himself was stricken, but he recovered.

In between epidemics, Deveaux had a happy home life. In 1872 he married the former Fannie Moore of Savannah, and they had five children.

In 1875, John Deveaux helped organize the *Savannah Tribune*, one of the oldest black newspapers in the state, and he served as editor and business manager until 1890. In his editorials he often covered the subject of racial pride and urged interracial cooperation.

In his lifetime, Deveaux belonged to several organizations. He was one of the first black Masons in Georgia and was a founder of the Odd Fellows in Savannah. In addition, he was active with the First Battalion, Georgia State Troops, advancing through the ranks to lieutenant colonel. In recognition of this, he was often addressed as "Colonel Deveaux" in his later years.

Deveaux's illustrious career ended when he died suddenly in Savannah on June 9, 1909, at the age of sixty-one.

Ten

BESSIE JONES

A National Treasure

"**F**rom the peanut fields of southwest Georgia to Carnegie Hall!"

So read a newspaper clipping about Bessie Jones, a captivating, crowd-pleasing performer who focused new attention on Georgia's musical folklore and was one of the leading forces behind the famed Sea Island Singers.

Bessie was more than thirty years old when she moved to St. Simons Island from her native Dawson, in southwest Georgia, where she was born in the early 1900s. It didn't take her long to get involved with a group performing the old plantation songs of the coast. Together, they renewed the spirit of their ancestors in an outpouring of rhythm and melody that caught on with listeners and began to attract regional, then national, attention.

With their special brand of swaying, hand-clapping, and singing all around the notes with humming and "trimmins," the singers transfixed audiences in a maze of wonder and appreciation. But it would have been hard for them to explain exactly how they did it. It just came out naturally, a colorful blend of their African heritage and the sometimes mournful and emotional sounds of their slave ancestors.

Bessie spent years with this group, known at that time

as the Coastal Singers of St. Simons. Around 1948 they came to the attention of Alan Lomax, filmmaker, folklorist, and Library of Congress archivist. Lomax was so taken with the group that he encouraged them to travel and display their unique style of folk harmonies to wider audiences. In 1948 they were formally organized as the Sea Island Singers, with Lomax as their producer.

In the succeeding years they toured widely, appearing at the prestigious Newport Festival in Rhode Island, and a variety of other folk festivals. They performed at Rockefeller Center and also mounted the stage at leading universities to entertain the students. With Lomax they recorded a special album called *Southern Journey* and made a documentary film for Georgia Public Television. This was a full-color, 30-minute portrait of the group, not only showing them in performance but also digging into the cultural history of their music.

At one time the group contained four generations of Bessie's family, the youngest was her five-year-old grandson. The Singers benefited greatly when Doug and Frankie Quimby, Brunswick residents, joined them. (Frankie had once been married to Bessie's son.)

Harry Belafonte found them at the Newport Festival. Greatly intrigued, he boosted them and appeared with them a number of times. Through his promotional help, they made an appearance at Carnegie Hall.

In 1964, Bessie attended a two-week workshop at the Idyllwild Arts Foundation in California. As a direct outgrowth of this, she coauthored (with Bess Lomax Hawes) a book about her life and her music called *Step It Down.*

One key to Bessie's popularity was her voice, which was deep and rich, with a quality like oozing honey. Emotions were stirred as she sang the timeless melodies. "There's something in the old spirituals that makes you warm," she once said.

In 1982, Bessie was one of fifteen master folk artists to receive a National Heritage Fellowship from the National Endowment for the Arts in Washington. The award was

Bessie Jones
[Courtesy Rev. G. L.
Jones]

presented during the Festival of American Folklife. Included was a cash award of $2,500 and hearty recogni-
tion of her fifty years of singing her very special brand of
music.

Bessie died in 1984 at the age of eighty-two. Her work
carries on, however, because of the movement she started.
Each August the Sea Island Singers hold a festival that
reminds people anew of the ageless heritage of Georgia's
traditional folk music.

ELEVEN

WILLIAM BARTRAM

Pioneer Naturalist of the Southeast

William Bartram was Georgia's first conservationist and ecologist as well as, you might say, the first touring camper.

He paddled up the majestic Altamaha, got lost with hearty good humor, and chronicled reptiles, birds, fish, gators, beaches, lagoons, and marshes—all with a grace and enthusiasm that has lost little in more than two hundred years. Furthermore, he did it before roads, cars, roadmaps, motels, air conditioning, and the loving attention of farmers' daughters!

A shy Quaker naturalist, William wandered through the Southeast between 1773 and 1778 to observe a great variety of flora and fauna, noting with an appraising eye everything he encountered. His book, *Travels of William Bartram*, was published in 1791. It was highly popular then, and has remained so ever since.

For two centuries readers have been inspired by the eloquent prose of Bartram and thrilled at the wonders he noted in his travelogue. Some modern readers, captivated by the melodic cadences of his Thoreau-like interpretations, have even attempted to retrace his route.

Observing the coastlands at twilight, he noted: "The glorious sovereign of day, rolling in on his gilded chariot, hastened to the western realms. Skies are serene and calm, the air temperately cool with gentle zephyrs breathing through the fragrant pines; the prospect around is enchantingly beautiful."

When it was time to tie up his boat after a river trip, he said, "I spread my blanket by my cheerful fire under the protecting shade of the hospitable live oak. I listened, undisturbed, to the divine hymns of the feathered songsters of the groves, while the softly whispering breezes faintly died away."

Bartram said at one point that he heard thousands of birds overhead, "making a sound like the roll of muffled drums as their wings beat the air."

Bartram's influence has been considerable in several ways. He was the first to make an orderly classification of plants and wildlife on the eastern coast, but he was more than just a naturalist. He was literary trailblazer, for the grandeur of his rolling prose influenced other writers to no small degree. Wordsworth and Coleridge would borrow phrases from him, and Thomas Carlisle praised him.

He was elated with each new discovery of plants and animals. Classifying them (using their scientific names) in his journal, his words remain readable and our interest is held. His technical accounts are balanced with plenty of warm, human observations.

Exploring St. Simons Island, he came to a farm whose owner lay on a bearskin smoking his pipe. The man said, "Welcome, stranger! I am indulging in the rational dictates of nature, taking a little rest, having just come in from the chase and fishing."

Bartram buffs can be found in many places outside Georgia and Florida, the two states he had the most to say about, Savannah, however, is headquarters for the Bartram Trail Conference, which includes adherents in the eight states visited by the naturalist: North and South Carolina, Georgia, Florida, Alabama, Mississippi, Louisiana and Tennessee.

The membership, comprising a wide variety of nature lovers, delights in looking for such diverse things as rare trees, habitats, or geologic formations. They are finding that everything Bartram was attracted to has significance today.

In their field trips, these members carry on the Bartram heritage by advocating protection of the outdoors. To date, they have installed more than fifty trail markers, mostly in Florida. In these locations they are often able to convince local authorities to set land aside for a park or nature area.

One can only wonder exactly what went through the mind of William Bartram, a scientist and a poet, as he first viewed the coastal islands of Georgia. Luckily we have his book to take us there, in mind and spirit.

TWELVE

LYDIA PARRISH

Preserver of Slave Songs

It's almost impossible to set old slave songs to music. There are tones you can't find on conventional scales, a lot of humming is involved, and emphasis is often in odd places. Furthermore, the slaves would embellish—decorating one prominent note with a variety of small notes they called "trimmins."

But Lydia Parrish made up her mind to preserve those old plantation songs anyway and get them down on paper. With determination, this St. Simons Island winter resident set about winning the trust of the blacks. In effect, she persuaded them to sing and dance for her.

Lydia, born in New Jersey in 1872, first came to the island in 1922. Her husband was Maxfield Parrish, a noted artist whose credits included children's books and covers for leading magazines. Because she liked the island better than he did, they worked out an agreement. After he did a couple of paintings inspired by this locale, he never came back. Lydia, on the other hand, spent every winter on St. Simons for forty years.

Lydia bought a house on the old Kelvin Grove property near Bloody Marsh. She found herself fascinated by the musical heritage of the islands, especially the antebellum songs handed down by successive black generations. Lydia was sure these old songs would be lost if someone

Lydia Parrish was dedicated to the faithful preservation of the old slave songs of the Sea Islands.

didn't get them written down. She became obsessed with the prospect of preservation.

It took imagination and persistence, but Lydia worked out a plan. Patiently, she coaxed and bribed a number of men and women, whose ancestors had worked in the cotton fields, to gather at a cabin near her property. Reluctant at first, these blacks began to sing and dance on a regular basis, making the cabin ring with their colorful rhythms.

By 1935 she had advanced the cause enough to permit an agreement with Alfred ("Bill") Jones of Sea Island to stage performances in the lobby of the Cloister Hotel. The concerts became popular and the Cloister even guaranteed, at each performance, a minimum of fifteen dollars for the group if the actual money collected failed to reach twenty dollars.

Included in the original group were Peter Davis, Ben Davis, and John Davis. Although Lydia didn't know it, she was starting a movement that would contribute directly to the formation of the famed Sea Island Singers. (Bessie Jones, an early mainstay of the singers, joined the group somewhat later.)

Lydia worked on the project for years and finally, in 1942, came a triumph. Her book, *Slave Songs of the Georgia Sea Islands*, was published by Creative Age Press of New York. It was based on her extensive notes and assisted diligently by a few of the more knowledgeable black performers. Music was faithfully copied out by two professionals, Creighton Churchill and Robert Mac-Gimsey.

The formal organization of the Sea Island Singers took place in 1948. Once this talented group caught on with audiences, they began appearing on concert stages from Canada to Mexico, and singing with Indians, cowboys, and bluegrass and country singers. They caught the attention of Harry Belafonte, who helped promote them, and they appeared at Carnegie Hall.

Unfortunately, Lydia Parrish did not live to see the

success of the singers. She died March 29, 1953, at the age of 81.

However, one sign of the significant contribution of this dedicated lady is the existence of a great annual festival. Thanks to her promptings and encouragement, what started as "happy moods of song" way back in the 1930s led to the formation, in 1974, of the Sea Island Festival. Today it is one of the peak events of the year in the Golden Isles.

THIRTEEN

ROBERT S. ABBOTT

From Humble Beginnings to Publishing Fame

On the grounds at Fort Frederica, St. Simons Island, stands an unusual monument. It's an obelisk, inscribed as follows: "In loving memory of my father and aunt, Thomas Abbott and Celia Abbott."

The story behind the monument is one of struggle, dedication, and rags-to-riches achievement. It was erected by Robert S. Abbott, founder and publisher of the Chicago *Defender*, a world-renowned black weekly newspaper. At its peak, it had a circulation of 225,000, with an estimated actual readership of 1,200,000 worldwide. The *Defender* was said to be the greatest achievement in the history of black journalism.

Robert Abbott was born on St. Simons Island on November 28, 1868, only a few years after the end of the Civil War. Both his parents were former slaves; his father died while Robert was still a baby and his mother, Flora Abbott, then married Rev. J. H. H. Sengstacke, a Congregational minister and German scholar.

Robert found himself in the loving care of his stepfather and was greatly influenced by this German newcomer, a multitalented fellow who had been, at various times, a teacher, minister, store owner, and publisher. He worked

*Robert S. Abbot,
founder and pub-
lisher of* The Chicago
Defender. *His news-
paper's circulation
grew to 225,000, with
an estimated read-
ership of 1,200,000.*

with the boy to develop a sense of racial pride, and planted
in his mind the widespread possibilities of a national
newspaper for blacks.

Robert grew up in Savannah, receiving a better-than-
average education, then going on to Claflin College in
South Carolina and Hampton Institute (now a university)
in Virginia. His summers were given performing odd jobs
at a Savannah newspaper. After graduation from Hampton in 1896 with a major in printing, he went back to
Savannah to work for his stepfather in publishing the
Woodville *Times.*

Hungering for still more education, Abbott entered
Kent College of Law in Chicago, from which he received
a law degree in 1898. At this point, friends warned him
that he would encounter prejudice if he set up a practice
in Chicago, so he returned to journalism.

In 1905, with capital of twenty-five cents, borrowed resources, and an agreement to pay printing costs after
sales, he published his first issue of the Chicago *Defender.* It was a feeble, four-page, 16- x 20-inch effort,

peddled door to door by a determined fellow who was editor, business manager, and entire staff, working out of the kitchen of the cheap apartment where he lived. In spite of tremendous obstacles Abbott would not be defeated; he trudged daily through snow, sludge, and mud, selling to homes, barbershops, churches, and pool halls. Gradually his circulation increased.

From the start the *Defender* took a stand for black rights. Its editorial creed was to "fight against segregation and discrimination until these evils have been removed." The paper played a prominent role in encouraging blacks to leave the South during and after World War I and to come north to seek better jobs.

In 1935 when the paper observed its thirtieth anniversary, Abbott wrote a "looking back" editorial, which said in part:

> Thirty years have passed since I began the publication of the Chicago *Defender.* I was editor, publisher, printer, and newsboy—going out in all kinds of weather. My friends made fun of me; they ridiculed me and laughed at me for they thought it was foolish to anticipate success in a field where so many before me had failed. But I went on fighting against what seemed insuperable odds; fighting the opposition of my adversaries on the one hand and the indifference of my *friends* on the other. A struggle out of which I emerged victorious, though battle-scarred.
>
> I entered the field of journalism with a determination to take the Negro newspaper out of the soap-wrapper class—to give the people a paper they would not be ashamed to read on the street cars, and which could not be put away like a dime novel in an inside pocket.
>
> I built up the *Defender* not only by printing all the news, but also by clinging to the idea that success could be achieved by recording contemporary documents and public utterances— and by contending for social justice, political rights, and industrial equity.
>
> They told me it could not be done; they said I could not own a commercial press. I couldn't do this; I couldn't do that. But today I own two commercial presses, and the circulation of

the *Defender*, prior to the Great Depression, was over a quarter of a million.

In truth, the newspaper had grown enough to make Abbott a millionaire. He lived well, traveled widely, and championed various minority issues. His contemporaries began calling him "the dean of Negro journalists."

In 1930 the successful editor introduced *Abbott's Monthly*, a magazine for blacks with a vivid four-color cover, which sold for twenty-five cents. In his monthly, Abbott included special features, romance stories, poems, jokes, book reviews, and cartoons. This seemed to go well at first, but later the magazine, a predecessor of *Ebony*, began to lose circulation. The problem was that Abbott had tried to include something of interest for everyone and it was too cluttered, lacking in direction and focus. It was discontinued in 1933.

But the *Defender* continued, slimmer than its former over-200,000 circulation, but still successful. Abbott was proud of it. A friend who often went to the theater with him once said that on their way home from the show Abbott would purposely drive past the newspaper's offices to just park and look. "In a way, he seemed surprised that it was still there," said his friend.

In the early thirties, Abbott erected the monument at Fort Frederica, near the site of the slave quarters where his father had passed his youth. The inscription was meant to be a fond remembrance of him and of two of Abbott's aunts (the other aunt is mentioned in a smaller plaque on the side of the obelisk). Abbott's mother, Flora Sengstacke, was a loyal colleague and workmate in the publishing business for many years. She passed away in 1932.

When Abbott died in 1940 at the age of seventy-one, he was mourned by thousands. His permanent memorial continues to be the Chicago *Defender*, now a daily newspaper with a circulation of approximately 25,000.

FOURTEEN

JOHN MCINTOSH KELL

Confederate Naval Hero

The lure of salt water was strong for John McIntosh Kell as he grew up near Darien, Georgia. His love of boats, in fact, was so powerful that none of his friends was surprised when, at age eighteen, he applied to be a midshipman in the U.S. Navy. He was accepted and then graduated from the Naval Academy in 1848.

Kell was a descendant of the original Scotch Highlanders of Darien. Born in 1823 at Laurel Grove plantation, he was a healthy lad who loved the woodlands and especially the tidewater creeks and marshes. The site of his old family home, a wooded area adjacent to Highway 99, is identified by a historic marker.

As a midshipman in the Federal Navy, Kell received a thorough grounding in seamanship. He rose through the ranks to lieutenant, traveling widely and seeing quite a bit of geography. He was with Commodore Perry on the latter's historic voyage to the Far East in 1853, which opened up Japan for world trade.

When Georgia seceded from the Union in 1861, Kell resigned his commission. With his experience, he was a valuable addition to the infant Confederate navy and he was gratified to receive orders to report to New Orleans for duty under Comdr. Raphael Semmes. He was chosen as

Semmes's executive officer, first on the *Sumter*, then on another Confederate raider, the CSS *Alabama*, a ship that would make history.

As second in command of the *Alabama*, Kell was involved in anticommerce activities over many miles of ocean. The ship was a pioneer in the concept of "commerce warfare," at which Germany was so adept in two world wars.

For almost two years the vessel roamed international waters, terrorizing Union merchant vessels from the Far East to the North Atlantic. Because of the Union blockade, it could never put into a Confederate port; the closest it came was an attack off Galveston, where it sank the USS *Hatteras* in a smoky, thirteen-minute encounter, the only time a rebel raider sank a U.S. warship.

Records show that the *Alabama* covered 75,000 miles, capturing well over 400 Yankee supply ships. Some fifty-five of these were destroyed, and something like $5.1 million in supplies were seized—greatly valuable cargo for the South.

Kell was always loyal to Semmes, the ultimate tactician who was fully the master of his ship and surely an inspirational leader. At one point, when the skipper made a daring escape, Kell is reported to have muttered, "Old Beeswax! What a seaman! I do believe he could navigate a washtub in a storm on the high seas!" (With affection, the men called Semmes "Old Beeswax" because of his mustache, which was waxed and curled at the ends.)

It was a dark day for the *Alabama* on June 19, 1864, when she was challenged by the USS *Kearsarge* off Cherbourg in the English Channel. French sightseers, lured by the impending sea battle, came from miles around. They saw a tremendous duel in which the two ships circled each other and fired salvos. Finally, the *Alabama* was sunk, but Kell, Semmes, and many in the crew were rescued by the welcome intervention of a British yacht.

After returning to the Confederacy, Kell was given command of the ironclad *Richmond* on the James River in

Virginia. Not long afterwards he was stricken with fever and sent home to recuperate; he was still there when the war ended and he never returned to sea.

Kell's postwar life was happy. For many years he supported his family as a farmer in Sunnyside, Georgia. During this time a friendship developed between the Kell family and Sidney Lanier, the famous poet. On many occasions, Lanier played his flute and recited his poetry in the parlor of the Kell home.

In 1886, Gov. John B. Gordon named Kell adjutant general of the state. The appointment focused new attention on the old war hero, to the enlightenment of a new generation of Georgians. He served with distinction for fourteen years.

When Kell died in 1900 at the age of seventy-seven, he was one of the most respected figures in the state.

FIFTEEN

CHICHOTA

The Goulds at Home

With paws clasping mighty shields, the massive stone lions face the marsh defiantly. They seem oddly out of place until the viewer learns that the ruined foundation behind them, over which they stand guard, is all that's left of the Edwin Gould cottage, Chichota, on Jekyll Island.

There are memories in that crumbling foundation and maybe that's why the fierce sentinels are so vigilant. Here there was romance, family bliss, carefree abandon, and stark tragedy.

In 1901 Edwin and Sarah Gould purchased a cozy bungalow in the Millionaire's Village and called it Chichota, which is thought to be the name of an ancient Creek Indian chief. Edwin, 35, a son of flamboyant Jay Gould, financier and railroad proprietor, had joined the Jekyll Island Club in 1899. The couple had two sons, Edwin Gould, Jr., and Frank Miller Gould.

Unlike his father, Edwin was a quiet, private person, hardly a ruthless business tycoon. Sporting a trim beard and looking like a thoughtful teacher or banker, he assumed the duties of trusteeship over his father's $80 million estate. By shrewd management, however, he amassed a fortune of his own and was generous to many charitable causes.

Fierce sentinels of the Gould family secrets, the two
stone lions are still on guard at the ruins of the Gould
Cottage on Jekyll Island. [Courtesy Jekyll Island
Museum]

Edwin and Sarah ("Sally") loved to leave New York and come to tranquil Jekyll Island, being especially entranced by their one-story, villa-type home facing the marsh, which housed an indoor swimming pool. Their marriage was a happy one and they were devoted to their two sons. In their island retreat they could rear them in relative safety, away from the hazards and distractions of the big city.

But in some ways, it seems, the Goulds were overprotective of the children. There were many activities—tennis, nature hikes, pony rides, and swimming—but always a watchful governess followed close behind the little ones, monitoring everything they did.

It didn't take Edwin long to buy up land adjacent to Chichota and begin making improvements. First he ordered the construction of an elaborate private wharf and boat dock. In 1902 he built a "casino," an immense structure which contained a bowling alley, a shooting gallery, and a game room. Later, he expanded this building and put in the island's first indoor tennis court.

But Edwin wasn't through making changes in the Jekyll landscape. When a large cottage was constructed behind Chichota, no one was surprised to find he had ordered it built for his in-laws, whom he had proposed for club membership. Accordingly, Dr. and Mrs. George Frederick Shrady, Sally's parents, moved into their handsome, two-story home in 1904. This cottage, later named Cherokee, became, in the 1990s, the headquarters of the Jekyll Museum and Historical Center.

Indeed, few unhappy events marred the Goulds' carefree days. One occurred in 1912, however, when Edwin was stricken by an epidemic of typhoid fever. For long weeks he hovered between life and death, but he eventually recovered.

Then on February 24, 1917, tragedy struck hard. Young Edwin, Jr., then in his mid-twenties, went out with a friend to check his wildlife traps on a nearby marshy island. When he found a raccoon in one of the traps, Gould decided not to shoot the animal and damage the skin but to club it with the butt of his shotgun. Unfortunately, when he did so the gun went off, killing him instantly.

Naturally, his parents were devastated. Sally's sorrow was such that she never again set foot on the island. Edwin, tormented by memories, came only occasionally and as the years passed did little to maintain the property. After he died in 1933 at the age of sixty-seven, Chichota remained vacant until it was torn down in 1940.

Perhaps those stone lions remember the good times enjoyed by a loving family in the old days. But they aren't talking.

SIXTEEN

BUMPS IN THE NIGHT
Resident Ghosts

Ghost stories abound in the Golden Isles and a collection of lore would not be complete without mentioning a few.

Generations of history (and mystery) set the scene. The parade of characters includes Guale Indians, Spaniards, pirates, English soldiers, planters, slaves, and assorted others. Their stories and legends have been handed down, telling of triumphs, tragedies, bloody battles, and sudden death—the stuff of which chilling tales are woven. Even the landscape provides an eerie ambience. Spanish moss on the century-old oaks, looking like a hangout of Satan's laundry, filters the moonlight down to the uneasy watcher below.

Then, too, the beaches add to the mystique. Phosphorescence dances on the waves, while a moonlit path leads across the water to Neptune's spectral temple. Palm fronds rustle, as ghostly crabs scurry across the sand. Overhead floats the tingling obligato of the watchful night birds.

Long before the Civil War the scene was set there for phantom doings. Slaves, bringing accounts of "h'ants" or "fixuhs" from Africa, talked often of visitations by spirits. "Just superstitions," said plantation owners, but were they? Who is to say where reality and legend merge?

If someone died in a house, it was said, you must not remove the body until a preacher said a few words; otherwise it would surely bring a "h'ant" to hover, perhaps for years. You could protect your dwelling from spirits by painting blue around the doorway.

For some, a paranormal attribute was a vested thing, the slaves believed. A baby born with a caul, or membrane, over its face would have special powers and be able to see ghosts. In others, there might be a different manifestation of the other dimension, such as the ability to cast spells. Conjure, for example, was deep magic; if you were born with it you'd have power over inanimate things such as sticks and roots and perhaps be able to cast spells on other people.

For years, Dunbar Creek on the west side of St. Simons Island has preserved a haunted reputation. It was here that a slave ship landed its cargo, a boatload of humanity from the Ebo (also called Ibo) tribe in what is now Nigeria. While chained together and about to be taken to the cotton fields for a life of bondage, their leader stirred them to drastic action. The group of slaves turned to the nearby stream and marched in, chanting, "The water brought us and the water will take us away." They drowned themselves, rather than submit to servitude.

Ever since that day, goes the legend, you can hear chanting, moaning, and the rattling of chains near the bluff adjacent to the sewage treatment plant at Dunbar Creek. To this day, there are those who avoid Ebo Landing after dark.

It's generally accepted among ghost hunters that a death, especially a sudden or violent one, can cause a haunting, for the spirit remains trapped at that one spot and cannot move on. There is uneasy evidence of this at an old home in McIntosh County.

Dating from the administration of George Washington, the venerable structure near Darien was built around 1790 and has been owned by the d'Antignac family (pronounced *Dant*-knack) since 1910. Jack and Debi d'Antignac, the present owners, are in the shrimping business. They share their home with a friendly "something" who, every now and then, gives an indication of his presence.

There's plenty of other history connected with their home. In 1820, for example, there was a plot to smuggle Napoleon out of St. Helena, where he'd been exiled, to America. French sympathizers had selected three locations in the United States, and one of them was the house in McIntosh County. The scheme fell through when the "Little Corporal" died in 1821, before the plan could be implemented. (The house was also a boyhood home for one Thomas Goulding, author, clergyman, and inventor of an early sewing machine.)

Then there's Brewster.

William Brewster was a doctor, clergyman, and occasional mortician who lived there in the early 1800s, said to have been hanged in the front yard for some unknown crime. Other accounts say he died in an upstairs bedroom. Either way, it's certain that he died there, and his spirit is apparently still vigilant.

The most eerie sighting of Dr. Brewster took place when his apparition was seen in broad daylight by two brothers, Jack d'Antignac's father and uncle, who were sitting on the front porch. As they talked, a man approached, walking from the direction of the nearby marsh. He was tall, with what appeared to be blond or silvery hair, and he wore a high, old-fashioned collar and a long, odd-looking coat. He seemed as solid as anybody else, but the brothers realized, as he drew near, that a part of him just wasn't there. His legs, below the knees, were not visible. The figure came up the front steps, entered the house, and climbed the stairs. He was probably heading for what is believed to be "Brewster's room," a bedroom from which noises occasionally erupt, such as footsteps and furniture being moved around.

The two men, speechless and quite shaken, didn't tell anybody about this for a long time.

Brewster has been known to squeeze people's toes

while they are reading in bed, but this stops when they turned off the light. Sometimes a toilet flushes—all by itself.

On one occasion the house's decrepit wiring shorted out in a roof section, almost causing a fire. A fire inspector, examining it later, related that the dry wood next to the frayed wiring had started to burn, but that something had put it out. "I can't understand it," he said. "This sort of electrical failure, with such tinder-dry beams, would be sure to cause a bad fire. And yet *something* stopped it before it could spread."

Brewster, nowadays, seems to be pretty quiet. He apparently lives in harmony with Debi, Jack, teenage daughter Beth, and Bosun, the aging family dog. They feel safe, even comfortable, knowing that the old family spook is a dedicated and loving protector of the family.

One of the most cherished ghost stories of St. Simons Island is the saga of Mary the Wanderer (or, in Geechee dialect, "Mary-de Wanda").

Does the specter of a lovely young girl with long flowing hair and sorrowful eyes still roam the beaches at the south end of the island? Many say they have seen her with her lantern held high, waiting and watching for the lover who went off to the mainland and never came back.

The young man, said to be a son of the Demere family, had quarreled with his father that morning. He shoved off in a rowboat, not knowing that hurricane-force winds were about to hit the islands. All day the storm raged and that night, when there was a lull, the girl started her agonized vigil. To her horror, she found his capsized boat, half-submerged beneath the waves. Distraught with grief, she cast herself into the foaming waters.

Some say Mary the Wanderer is still watching and waiting, especially on stormy nights. Sometimes, when sighted, she carries a lantern; sometimes she appears in a white, shroudlike garment.

One who encountered Mary years ago was Carolyn Butler, a former third-grade teacher at St. Simons Elementary School. The thing Carolyn saw wasn't human in form—it was more like a big white blob—but it put a tremendous fear into both her and her dog, Boots, who ran away from home as a result. "You just know when you've seen a ghost," she said. "You've never been colder in your life and then you break out in heavy perspiration."

Another sighting, believed to be Mary, was experienced by John Symons and his wife, longtime island residents. The two were restless on a hot night (before the days of air-conditioning) and went off for a cooling automobile ride around 2 A.M. As they were heading south on the airport road, a surprising sight suddenly appeared along-side the road. It was a woman, wearing what looked like a white veil, standing in front of a horse. They both saw her.

Just at that minute the car windows fogged over with icy mist, an impossibility on such a warm night. John had to open the door and put his head out to see any-thing, and, as he slowed the car, he looked back. For a moment the horse and woman were visible and then, in an instant, they both disappeared. It took the two quite a while to stop shivering from the experience.

Even more bizarre is the story of the plane making an approach one evening at McKinnon Airport. Tower per-sonnel were shocked when the pilot suddenly called them, "There's a woman and a horse on the runway!" This brought a reply, in disbelief, from the tower, "Well, you'd better circle and come in again." On the next ap-proach, the woman and horse were gone.

Another of St. Simons's well-known ghost stories, wit-nessed by many over the years, is the tale of the light in the churchyard. Years ago, an island woman was terribly afraid of the dark and always slept with a lighted candle by her bed. She kept a large inventory of beeswax candles handy for use. Then she passed away and was buried at Christ Church.

Her husband couldn't stop thinking of his wife, who so feared the dark in her lifetime, lying alone in the dark churchyard. Therefore he placed a lighted candle on her tombstone, a practice he continued for many years, until it became something of a local landmark.

After he died, the flickering candle did not vanish. It could be seen among the headstones and people passing would watch for it. The ghost, it seems, never disappointed sightseers. They would drive slowly down the road, lights dimmed to watch for that ghostly glimmer. Suddenly there it was, and it would always thrill those watching, even the skeptics among them.

Up and down the Georgia coast you'll find many happenings that can't be explained rationally. The historic community of Midway in Liberty County, for example, has had a few ghosts prowling about in its more than 200 years of existence. One of the often-told stories is that of the crack in the wall of the old Midway cemetery.

Found at the northeast corner of the brick wall of the cemetery, the crack was *not* made by human hands, they say. It's the manifestation of a ghastly deed.

The wall was built by slaves, and one day two of them quarreled. Their overseer noted that the pair had not finished their work and, as punishment, ordered them to work overtime. That night one of the men killed the other with a brick. The murderer buried his victim under the foundation of the wall. Carefully, he replaced the brickwork, hoping no one would discover his crime. He then told his master that his companion had run away.

Shortly afterward, a large crack appeared in the wall at the scene of the murder. It was mended, only to crack again. This happened repeatedly. Years later the bones of the dead slave were found but the brickwork kept rupturing, as if the spirit of the victim could not rest. For years, afterwards, descendants of the slaves would say, "Ain't no use to mend it. It's gonna crack as fast as it gets fixed."

Travel upriver on the Altamaha and you'll come to Hannah's Island, near Doctortown, where there's another spine-tingling bit of ghostly lore.

During the Civil War a woman named Hannah was killed in a sudden act of violence. Later, in the postwar era, big timber rafts would be floated down the river, taking Georgia yellow pine to the mills at Darien. As they passed, crewmen would be awestruck by the misty, glowing figure of a woman, standing at the shore of the island and calling out to them, "Throw me the rope, boy."

Cumberland Island has its secrets, too. Folks visiting the grand old Dungeness mansion (once owned by a Carnegie) have, at times, heard the creaking of wooden wheels coming down the driveway. Long ago, says the island tale, a carriage filled with guests was coming to the mansion for a party. There was an accident and the wagon was wrecked. Ever since, spirits of the lost souls killed in the mishap have been trying to get to the party.

Another tale, still remembered in St. Marys, concerns the headless ghost of the Ross Inn. This old hostelry, which was destroyed by Hurricane Dora in 1964, had a secret passage connecting two of the rooms on the upper floor, which expedited the robbing of guests while they slept, a not-too-infrequent occurrence.

The Ross Inn's resident ghost, a headless form seen on many occasions, was supposed to be the apparition of a pirate. During excavations after the inn was leveled by the hurricane, a skeleton, minus a head, was uncovered. One account is that the pirate was beheaded during the Revolution. He kept returning, all through the years, to search for his missing body part.

Overall, the coastal ghosts are a peaceful sort, with some of them seeming to be watchful and protective. It's hard to find malevolent spirits in the area and there is little evidence of those nuisance ghosts called poltergeists, who move things and make noises.

Why are the local apparitions so docile?

Maybe it's the slow pace, the tranquil lifestyle, which has transferred from the earthly realm to the beyond.

SEVENTEEN

GEORGIANS IN TINSELTOWN
A Hollywood Who's Who

In the film *Gentlemen Prefer Blondes*, Marilyn Monroe meets a plump, well-heeled Casanova and is immediately attracted to his bankroll. She looks at Piggy, played by Charles Coburn, sees a huge diamond materializing out of his head, and makes herself available to this Lothario of the Riviera, leading to many uproarious situations.

Although Marilyn and Jane Russell had leading parts, Coburn stole the show. The Savannah native was known for witty, erudite roles, often playing a rich uncle or monocled British aristocrat. He was one of Hollywood's premier character actors.

Coburn was already a stage veteran when he decided to go to the film capital in the 1930s. He appeared in light comedies and lent character support in such movies as *The Green Years, King's Row*, and *The More the Merrier*, for which he won an Oscar. He never forgot his native state, however; in later years he came back for a series of lectures at the University of Georgia and donated the Coburn Collection to the university: an assortment of costumes, playbills, and scrapbooks.

Many Georgians have made their mark in Tinseltown,

Charles Coburn, a native of Savannah, was a much-in-demand character actor. [Courtesy Famous Photo Gallery]

and Coburn isn't the only one who hailed from the coastal area. Another was Jim Brown, who was born on St. Simons Island but moved to Long Island, New York, at the age of nine. He starred in several sports at Manhasset High School, then played football at Syracuse University, where he gained All-American honors.

Jim played pro football with the Cleveland Browns, establishing several records, including an amazing 1,863 yards gained in a single season. He was elected to pro football's Hall of Fame in 1971, the first year of his eligibility.

After the 1965 season, he left the sport to accept a movie role. Some of his many films include *The Dirty Dozen, Ice Station Zebra,* and *I Escaped from Devil's Island.*

Jim has done a lot to improve economic opportunities for blacks in America, serving as founder of the National Negro Industrial and Economic Union.

Pernell Roberts, a native Waycross, joined the Marine Corps after graduation from Waycross High School. Then he found himself strongly drawn to the theater and serve his apprenticeship on Broadway. This led to a brief movie appearance in *Desire under the Elms,* playing Tony Perkins's older brother. Some television work followed, and Pernell's big break came when he was selected to play the part of Adam Cartwright in "Bonanza." He left the show after six years to seek wider horizons.

After a few movie roles, he returned to TV for the lead in "Trapper John, M.D." in 1979. Roberts has distinguished himself in a number of other roles since then.

Not many know that one of the greatest of movie funnymen, Oliver Hardy, came from Georgia. He was born in Harlem, just outside Augusta, in 1892.

The corpulent Hardy had show business in his blood, so he dropped out of law school and went to Jacksonville, a center for filming two-reel comedies. Success followed, and Hardy moved on to Hollywood to appear with Buster Keaton and others. Later he teamed up with former British circus performer Stan Laurel and movie history was made. The partnership yielded nearly ninety short comedies between 1926 and 1951; all told, Laurel and Hardy made more than 200 films.

In 1989, Harlem honored its native son with the first Oliver Hardy Film Festival. One of the enjoyable features is a dress-up contest in which portly look-alikes don derby hats and little square mustaches. But there's more: a parade, arts and crafts, clown acts, children's rides, and (of course) showings of some of Laurel and Hardy's greatest movies. The Oliver Hardy Museum contains memorabilia commemorating the two funnymen.

Among Georgians who made good in Hollywood, perhaps Burt Reynolds is best known. Born in Waycross, Burt left Georgia at an early age, moving with his family to West Palm Beach, Florida. Burt owes a lot to an early break when he was working at a playhouse in New York; his talent was noted by fellow Georgian Joanne Wood-

Although born in Waycross, Burt Reynolds moved to Florida at an early age. Burt has turned his back on Hollywood and makes movies in and around Jupiter, Florida. [Courtesy Famous Photo Gallery]

ward, and her tip to an agent led to better opportunities and eventually to leading roles.

A list of Burt's movies includes *Sharkey's Machine, Deliverance* (filmed in the rugged wilderness of northeast Georgia), and the popular *Smokey and the Bandit.* His most recent success is television's "Evening Shade."

Way back in the days of silent films, well before Gone With the Wind, Georgia's movie emissaries were making big splashes. A good reminder of this is a story from a 1924 edition of the Atlanta Journal by Margaret Mitchell, whose by-line was Peggy Mitchell. Under the headline "Movie Stars Who Make Atlanta Home," Peggy profiled Ben Lyon, Mabel Normand, Colleen Moore, and a smattering of bit players.

Came the Depression days and Atlanta-born Lee Tracy became a familiar name. He, too started on the stage; and, when he showed up in Hollywood, he was picked for a number of fast-talking roles, often playing a nosey reporter or a private detective. About the same time, Evelyn Keyes, another Atlanta product (although born in Texas) was attracting notice. In one of her best-remembered roles, Evelyn played Scarlett O'Hara's younger sister in *Gone With the Wind.*

Then there's that slim, five-foot-nine actress from Smyrna, next door to Atlanta. Julia Roberts's acting skill came quite naturally; her mother was a drama coach. Among her movies are *Steel Magnolias, Pretty Woman, Mystic Pizza,* and *The Pelican Brief.*

Leaving Atlanta, we come to Melvyn Douglas, who was born in Macon in 1902. After a stage apprenticeship, he graduated to the movies and became a suave leading man, playing opposite some of the best-known actresses of the era.

Speaking of leading ladies, let's not forget two who have gained international recognition, Miriam Hopkins and Joanne Woodward. Miriam, born in Savannah, grew up in Bainbridge and made her first movie in the early thirties after a long stage career. Probably her best known film credit was the title role in *Becky Sharp,* the first Technicolor movie. Joanne, born in Thomasville, studied dramatics in New York, then chalked up many stage successes, followed by movie stardom. She won an Oscar for *Three Faces of Eve* in 1957.

Kim Basinger was born in Athens in 1953. She began as a fashion model, then moved to California and landed a number of movie roles. In recent years, Kim has also headed an investment group that bought the little town of Braselton, near Athens. She planned to replace outmoded downtown stores with upscale boutiques and other business enterprises.

Then there are the nonactors who also did big things in the film industry. Lamar Trotti of Atlanta and Nunnally Johnson of Columbus were both leading writers and producers. Savannah-born Johnny Mercer, who occasionally

Bainbridge's most famous native daughter was Miriam Hopkins, a standout film star in the 1930s and 1940s. Miriam played the title role in Becky Sharp, *the first full-color movie.* [Courtesy Famous Photo Gallery]

appeared in supporting roles with such stars as Bing Crosby, was a famous lyricist, penning the words to such enduring songs as "In the Cool, Cool, Cool of the Evening," "Moon River," "Laura," and "That Old Black Magic."

Certainly many native Georgians found fame and fortune in Tinseltown, and we salute them for their solid contributions to American entertainment.

HISTORIC
HAPPENINGS

A scene looking south on Newcastle Street in Brunswick in the aftermath of the storm shows heavy roof damage to buildings (left) and horses wading in the flooded streets.

EIGHTEEN

HURRICANE WARNING

The Big Blow of 1898

It started in the Leeward Islands on September 25, 1898, that violent whirling of tropical winds that signals a hurricane. Slowly, relentlessly, it approached the Georgia coast.

In those days storms were not named as they are now but for years folks would remember this one as "the Big Blow of '98," a savage hurricane that left more than 100 dead.

A preview of the coming blast came days earlier with strong winds, heavy rains, and unusually high tides. Then the center of the hurricane struck on October 2. Although the main impact was just north of Brunswick, the backlash affected the entire seacoast, causing flooding and property damage over a wide area.

On St. Simons Island, youthful Horace Gould lived with his mother and sister. In a long letter, written later to a relative, he told of becoming alarmed by rising water. On Sunday morning, October 2, he checked the livestock and consoled himself with the thought that the water coming down the road would reverse when the tide turned. It didn't. In disbelief, he watched it come over the yard and approach the house, with the accompaniment of powerful gusts of wind.

Moments later what Horace had feared, the flooding of the lower parts of the house, became a reality. He wrote of rushing to the storeroom and lifting loose objects to higher shelves. Next, he herded the family pig to the kitchen porch and put some of the chickens under the stove. As the water rose in the kitchen he turned his attention to a desperate kitten, clinging to a floating box, and lifted it to a windowsill. Then he rescued the soggy chickens and perched them atop the stove; this, unfortunately, was not high enough and they were swept away. The boy and his mother and sister climbed to higher parts of the house.

Watching from an upper window, the three were dismayed to see their porch separating from the main part of their home. Soon it was churning away with the flood. "The yard," he related, "looked like the ocean with great waves chasing each other across from east to west." Animals and birds, in various stages of drowning, could be seen in the waters surging past. His mother caught two hens as they were passing and saved them.

Then suddenly the water began to recede. At about 3:00 P.M. the worst was over, and by evening the winds moderated to a gentle breeze.

The next morning, Horace surveyed the damage, which, he noted, was widespread over the island. Houses were uprooted and carried away, some with entire sides or roofs gone. Old oaks, prominent in his childhood memories, were flat on the ground; fragments of chairs, tables, linens, and crockery lay strewn about. Exhausted sea birds perched here and there amongst the bodies of dead animals. Fresh fruit, washed in from the sea, indicated cargo vessels lost near the coast.

In nearby Brunswick, the Union Depot was five feet under water, while docks and warehouses were damaged heavily or washed away. One resident measured six feet of water at the corner of Gloucester and Newcastle streets in the heart of town. Another man rowed a bateau downtown to check on his office. When he arrived, he was able to open the door and row right in!

Whereas most Brunswick residents took the storm seriously, others made sport of it. Small boys, for example, had a great time; after collecting logs they nailed strips across them to make rafts. Down in the toughest part of town near the waterfront, called "Hell's Half-Acre," there was a party atmosphere. Bedlam prevailed, complete with shouting, drinking, and even a shooting.

At the livery stable, rising floods threatened the horses, and one account tells of men "struggling and swimming into every stall with sharp knives to cut the beasts loose." Firehouse horses swam out of the station in eight feet of water; all over town efforts were made to move horses to high and dry places.

The Brunswick Baptist Church, one of the city's most imposing brick structures, became a temporary home for several mules, and the story goes that they showed their respect by eating the hymnals. Afterwards a wag remarked that "it wasn't the first time there was a jackass in the pulpit."

Men were seen carrying women and children to safety into the Mansfield Street School, which was another solid house of refuge. The tin roof was partly blown off, but from every window people were gazing anxiously at the flooded streets.

The correspondent for the Savannah *Evening News*, who had rushed to Brunswick, had a close call when his two horses sank into a hole, pulling his four-wheel carriage with them. The steeds were cut loose and swam out, and the carriage was later saved. The intrepid reporter, after getting the story, couldn't get out of town because of flood waters, nor could he use the telephone or telegraph because wires were down. Finally, with the help of Western Union technicians, broken lines were tapped and the outside world was informed.

A Jekyll Island old-timer recollected intense damage there, too. "Because of that hurricane," he said, "I spent the night up in a tree. It was the only tree on Jekyll that wasn't covered with ocean!" Nor was the famed Millionaire's Village spared. All the cottages were vacant with only caretakers in residence, and in a terse letter to the Jekyll Island Club president, the grounds superintendent reported that all the bridges, the pavilion, and the bath houses were carried away. "Portions of the wharf were found on Mr. Pulitzer's lawn," he said, adding that "the entire golf course is covered with tide water. I am afraid there will be no grass."

The town of Jesup presented a forlorn appearance the morning after the hurricane, with many streets impassable because of debris. Although many houses were damaged, none was blown down. In the surrounding forests, turpentine farmers were hit hard, and it was estimated that only one-fourth of the crop trees were left standing.

Farm buildings were flattened and livestock destroyed in several rural areas. Bridges were torn from their supports as far inland as Waycross, and damage to small boats, all along the coast, was especially high. On a branch of the Sapelo River, south of Savannah, people told of seeing dead horses floating down the stream, followed by a house with survivors on the roof.

Near Darien, a woman kept two children alive by sitting with them in the crotch of a tree until the storm subsided. Not so lucky were a man and his wife at Egg Island, just below Sapelo Island. The two were washed off their roof and the man, swimming to a nearby tree and holding fast to his wife, grasped a branch for support. He was unable to climb, so there he clung. His wife died in his arms and later was torn from his grasp. Then he, too, was swept away but saved himself by clutching a mass of floating debris where he stayed, more dead than alive. After three days he was picked up by a steamer, having drifted many miles out to sea.

Total cost of the storm was in the millions, including that year's cotton crop, which was ruined. Everywhere survivors lamented the lack of warning and being caught completely by surprise in an age when prompt, accurate weather forecasting was nonexistent.

The storm was thought to have included a tidal wave, but there was no single surge or wall of water, merely a rise from wind-sustained tides causing the highest water ever witnessed along that coast. It averaged five feet over the marshlands, while the greatest depth measured twelve feet.

There was a gubernatorial election the following week and voters were expected to stay away from the polls because of bad traveling conditions. The light vote and a new ballot-counting system allowed the citizens of Georgia to know within hours that Allen D. Candler had been elected governor.

The casualty count from the Big Blow, however, took longer. The death toll slowly mounted as bits of information leaked in, and it took a jump when the steamer *Hessie*, running out of Darien, discovered eighty bodies on Butler Island. Most of those killed were rice farmers, especially on the islands near the mouth of the Altamaha River.

One source gave the final count as 179 dead, making the Hurricane of 1898 one of the state's worst natural disasters.

NINETEEN

MIDWAY

From Early Turmoil to a Trail of History

Georgia history has its own famous cow, though it's not as well known as Mrs. O'Leary's, who is reported to have started the great Chicago fire by kicking over a lantern in the hay barn.

Late one evening in 1778, during the Revolutionary War, a lady named Amanda was milking her cow. This was at Midway in Liberty County, at a time when everybody was nervous because the British were at hand and might stage an attack at any time. Suddenly, Amanda looked up from her milking and saw two British soldiers setting fire to the church meetinghouse.

Amanda knew just what to do.

Not taking the time to get water from the well, she rushed over with her milking pail (after the men had gone) and doused the flames with milk. Then the soldiers returned to restart the fire. Again, Amanda put it out, using more of her precious milk.

When the soldiers came back once again, they discovered Amanda and put a stop to her efforts. The building burned to the ground.

It's a pity, said many folks, that Amanda's cow never had a monument dedicated to her.

It's hard to overlook the weight of the past in Midway. You get the feeling that there are age-old secrets here, a place where many generations worked, lived, and loved. That's what Midway is: old, revered, and unforgettable.

It all goes back to the late seventeenth century when a band of earnest Puritans started a congregation in Massachusetts. Later, they moved to Connecticut, then to South Carolina. This was not their final move, however, because their dissatisfaction with the land caused them to search out a new location for their flock in the 1750s. Having heard of the rich lands and agreeable climate in Georgia, they sent a delegation, in 1752, to "Midway, the place proposed." In a short time, more of these Protestant dissenters arrived, bringing their slaves. When fully established, there were probably 250 whites and around 1,500 blacks.

They liked the place from the start. It was midway between the Ogeechee and Altamaha rivers, hence the name. The ardent band had found a real home and they set about planting crops and building their dwellings.

The province at that time was divided into parishes and Midway, along with the seaport of Sunbury, just nine miles away, was in St. John's Parish. Records show that the two towns were closely associated and there was plenty of traffic between them.

For a long while things went well in this growing community. Among the early arrivals were Scottish Highlanders from Darien, just down the coast. These frugal newcomers were offsprings of the Scotch pioneers brought over from the Old Country by James Oglethorpe.

The history of Midway cannot be separated from that of the landmark church. First there was a rude pole structure, followed by the wooden edifice that Amanda's cow vainly tried to save. Finally, on the very same spot, the present-day church was erected in 1792. One of its distinctive features is a large gallery, designed to permit the slaves to attend services.

While religion was essential to these early Puritans, so

The historic Midway Church. This structure, replacing earlier church buildings, was built in 1792. [Courtesy Midway Historical Society]

was education. In 1788 they established the Sunbury Academy. Under the guidance of Dr. William McWhirr, an Irish scholar and a leader in improving the minds of citizens, the academy flourished. Many a Georgia plantation owner sent his sons to this school.

During the Revolution, British troops drove all the residents from their homes. When peace was declared, most of the planters came back to reclaim their lands.

Two of the most resolute patriots should be mentioned, and both became generals in the Colonial army. They were James Screven, a former captain of the body called St. John's Rangers, and Daniel Stewart, who served under General Marion, the Swamp Fox. Stewart was the great-grandfather of President Theodore Roosevelt. The marble shaft in the center of the churchyard cemetery was erected to the memory of these two soldiers by an act of Congress in 1915.

Of the three who signed the Declaration of Independence for Georgia, Lyman Hall (later a governor) and Button Gwinnett were from St. John's Parish. The list of other notables is impressive: doctors, teachers, merchants, lawyers, clergymen, and U.S. congressmen and senators. Because of the patriotic spirit of the people here and their inspiring service rendered to the cause of American independence, the county that later emerged here was named Liberty.

The Midway Society is composed of descendants of the original settlers and, although members are scattered geographically, it meets each year in April. With so much to be proud of, these "select men" gather to renew friendships, talk about their illustrious ancestors, and see what needs to be done to maintain the property and remind people of the old traditions.

TWENTY

SUNBURY

Forgotten Town of Liberty County

In his travels in 1773 William Bartram, the Quaker naturalist, stopped at what he called a "seaport town south of Savannah beautifully situated on the main."

He found an excellent harbor, suitable for "ships of great burden" and that evening he spent his time "in a circle of genteel and polite ladies and gentlemen."

Bartram had discovered Sunbury, now one of Georgia's long-lost eighteenth-century towns. While it prospered, it was home for several hundred, but by the time of the Civil War it was a ghost town and nothing remains today except the ruins of a nearby earthen fortification.

It all started in 1748 when Mark Carr petitioned Colonial authorities to form a community at a curve of the Medway River (old-style spelling), about eight miles upstream from St. Catherine's Island. Carr, also a pioneer of early Brunswick, was granted 1,000 acres, so he set up camp and persuaded others to join him. At first the place was called Captain Carr's Bluff, but the name was later changed to Sunbury in honor of Sunbury on the Thames River in England.

In 1752, a new group of settlers began arriving, taking

This is a portion of the moat surrounding the earth-works stronghold, Fort Morris. The fort was built to protect the town of Sunbury, of which no trace remains today. [Courtesy Georgia Department of Natural Resources]

up land grants a few miles away. These were Protestant dissenters from Dorchester, South Carolina, and they promptly built houses, a meeting hall, and a landmark church. By 1758 they had formed a bustling crossroads village called Midway, and there was much friendly communication between the two towns.

A master plan for Sunbury, drawn up in 1758, shows wharves for shipping, three public squares, and an ambitious layout of 496 home lots. It seemed ideal for a trad-

Visitors to the Sunbury-Fort Morris location are often treated to a re-enactment of camp life. Re-enactors camp out, cook their meals, sew and mend uniforms, and occasionally fight duels. [Courtesy Georgia Department of Natural Resources]

ing center and, indeed, as soon as docks were built, ships began to unload and pick up cargoes.

After a few years of growth, Sunbury rivaled Savannah in commercial importance, and some said it would grow to be much bigger. Exports at the time were staves, shingles, tanned leather, beef, pork, rice, corn, and indigo. Imports included rum, flour, apples, biscuits, cordials, and loaf sugar.

But Sunbury's growth was not entirely painless. In 1756 folks were terrorized by rumors of a hostile Creek Indian uprising, but this proved false. A plague swept the town in the late 1750s, causing several deaths.

Sunbury's most exciting times were during the American Revolution. To replace earlier fortifications, Congress authorized building a substantial fort to meet the British threat. Accordingly, an earthwork stronghold mounting twenty-five cannon was erected, commanding both land and water approaches. It was named Fort Morris, after Capt. Thomas Morris, the officer in charge.

The troops guarding Sunbury were reinforced by soldiers of the Third Georgia Battalion, under the command of Lt. Col. John McIntosh. It was this stubborn officer who, upon receiving demand for the fort's surrender from the approaching British, replied "Come and take it!" This brought an immediate assault by the Redcoats but it was unsuccessful. Later, British troops not only captured the fort but laid waste to the town.

After the Revolution, citizens who had fled came back and reconstruction was soon underway. Again, Sunbury began to thrive and its commerce returned to normal, continuing so into the nineteenth century.

Came the mid-1800s, however, and Sunbury experienced a serious population decline. Demand had fallen off for the area's rice crop, and the newly constructed railroads had bypassed the town in favor of other Georgia communities. Another factor was the force of nature. Hurricanes in 1804 and 1824 had caused widespread damage and misery.

In 1829 the population was down to 150; by 1855 there were only six or eight families left. When the Civil War started, once-proud Sunbury was a deserted village.

TWENTY-ONE

JEKYLL ISLAND

Gathering Place for the Affluent

During the glory days of the Jekyll Island Club where the world's heaviest money assembled, poker games took place regularly, but not for stakes. Members were not out to take each other's money; it was a sort of entrepreneurial competition to "test your aptitude for making money and succeeding in business."

One evening members at the poker table decided they didn't like the shrubbery around the clubhouse. The argument went on and on.

George F. Fabyan, a member from 1891 to 1907, listened impatiently. Finally he'd had enough.

"All right, gentlemen," he said, "let's all ante up $5,000 so we can buy some shrubbery. Then let's get on with the game!" They raised $30,000 on the spot to beautify the landscape. Such seemingly flamboyant occurrences were common when the millionaires got together at tranquil Jekyll Island in its most affluent heyday.

The year 1886 was a turning point in Jekyll's history. A group of millionaires, estimated to be in control of one-sixth of the world's wealth, bought the island for $125,000. These men were world-weary, longing to get away from the press of business and relax in luxury for three months of the year. In a short time, plans were under way for the erection of a rambling clubhouse and a number of modest "cottages," which were actually multiroom dwellings.

Liking what they had created, the titans planned docks and roads and also invited others (who were the right sort!) to join them. The exclusive Millionaire's Village, which became one of the most opulent, and certainly most exclusive, resorts in the world, was well on its way.

The members looked with lofty disdain on nonmembers who, regardless of who they were, were regarded as strangers. However, famous people who came to visit were welcomed, including Winston Churchill and President William McKinley. The membership roll was always guarded closely. There are stories of strange boats, approaching by sea, suddenly stopped by Jekyll guardian craft and told that no landing was permitted.

Although the clubhouse was functional, it was apparently not elaborate. There was no bar, for example, and drinks were served in a den in which the chief piece of furniture was a giant poker table. Inside the front door, it was said, were dozens of hooks with the names of the wealthiest men in the country under them. If one's name adorned the Jekyll Island Club hatrack, one had made it!

The original cottages contained no kitchens, for all cooking was done in the spacious kitchen of the clubhouse. Here, no expense was spared, for the head chef from Delmonico's restaurant in New York was lured to put together some of the most fabulous repasts in culinary history. It was not uncommon for these dinners to last three hours or more.

Joseph Pulitzer was a member who liked peace and quiet. The famous publisher was almost totally blind when he came to Jekyll, and he was so susceptible to noise that he demanded a fully soundproofed home. Once, when there was a dredge working in the river not far from his homesite, its steam whistle posed a problem.

The first Jekyll Island Clubhouse, designed by architect Charles A. Alexander and completed in 1887. Built in Queen Anne style, it was to be a "magnificent but not ostentatious" building. [Courtesy Jekyll Island Museum]

Pulitzer paid the dredge captain $100 a day to refrain from blowing the whistle.

It was said that the most significant event in the club's history occurred in 1910. A banking committee assembled at the island to brainstorm a few ideas that might prevent future financial panics. The financiers, some of the biggest men in banking, got together for ten days to discuss existing banking laws. Their monumental report became the Federal Reserve Bank Act.

As the millionaires' cottages kept going up, the moguls found themselves in a sort of competition. They tried to "one up" each other with the size of their cottages. The rivalry came to an end, however, when Richard Crane, the plumbing magnate, completed a mansion that had twenty-one bedrooms and seventeen baths, some reportedly having solid gold fixtures. This showplace cost $500,000 and was partially furnished with tables and benches from an Italian monastery.

By the Depression-ridden 1930s, Jekyll's heyday was fading. Other resorts were beckoning, and the younger crowd didn't have the same enthusiasm for the place. Then, too, when World War II got started, the need to disband the faltering club was real; German submarines had been operating near the island and government officials were worried about having such a concentration of the nation's financial might assembled in one vulnerable spot.

In addition, there were other problems brought on by the war. Travel was increasingly difficult, fuel was in short supply, and labor was both scarce and expensive as workers were being lured away by war industries. Somehow the club lasted for the 1942 season, but it didn't open in 1943, or ever again.

Today, Jekyll Island, with its modern motels, resorts, and golf courses, doesn't dwell much on its past. It's still a haven for the world-weary, but they come now to bask in the sunshine, swim, fish, or play eighteen holes. The millionaires' cottages are still there, now used for offices, exhibits, and galleries. By their presence they remind visitors of an opulent era of the past, when the best-bankrolled tycoons in the world gathered there.

TWENTY-TWO

ST. SIMONS

Digging Up Bones (and Other Ancient Island Relics)

Oscar didn't say anything much, but he sure grinned a lot. What could one expect? Oscar was no more than a skull found while ground was being cleared for the McKinnon Airport at St. Simons Island in the fall of 1935. He was named by the folks at the Brunswick Chamber of Commerce, where he was put on display. But it didn't take long before an archaeologist saw Oscar and said, "You better notify the Smithsonian Institution!"

So it was that a major dig began in May 1936. The county agreed to suspend construction of the airfield to give the scientists time for their search. The Smithsonian experts had decided also to examine Indian mounds at Gascoigne Bluff, Cannon's Point, and the northeast end of Sea Island, near the Hampton River.

The Great Depression was on, so workers were recruited through the WPA (Works Project Administration), which created jobs in tough times. This prompted a classic remark from an archaeologist, "The Depression, which resulted in so much unemployment, has done much for the history of primitive man!"

The big dig was sponsored by Glynn County and the Sea Island Company. With a daily audience of local citizens, long, narrow, chest-deep trenches severed the airport land-scape and exposed new treasures every few minutes. Un-covered was an ancient village site and burial ground. The evidence of clay floors pointed to a large number of dwell-ings, and more than 150 burials were uncovered. Artifacts indicated a prehistoric occupation well before A.D. 1500.

Many of the items found were believed to be special offerings, tucked away with the deceased to please the gods on his way to the Happy Hunting Grounds. These included weapons, tools, cooking pots, stoneware, bone awls, and thousands of shards (broken pieces of pottery).

Other interesting finds included: conch implements such as hoes and drinking cups, alligator tooth pendants, and polished flint arrowheads, which must have been brought from north Georgia as there is no flint native to the coast. Also found were a green sandstone charm, the ossified earbone of a whale, a clay turtle believed to have religious significance, and an earring made of copper, probably obtained by trading with northern tribes as it resembled copper items from the Lake Superior region.

At the Sea Island site a huge mound was thought to be the burial place for some sort of camp or seasonal village, which could have been a favorite fishing place in ancient times, as it is today.

One of the Sea Island skeletons wore an apron made of 225 olive shell beads; another skeleton was that of a young man less than twenty years old and six feet, five inches in height. This was a person of importance, per-haps the son of a chief, for his burial offerings were varied and numerous, including deer bone awls, unusual pen-dants, and a string of sea-snail shell beads.

The artifacts were classified by Smithsonian re-searchers as belonging to the Guale tribe of Coastal Creek Indians, although there were traces of the Timucuan tribe, associated with Florida.

Some of the 1936 archaeological finds were shipped to the Smithsonian Institution, but others were displayed locally, arousing the attention and wonder of local citizens.

TWENTY-THREE

CAMDEN COUNTY

The Heritage of Hunting

It's reported to be the first organized hunting club in America. True or not, the Camden Hunting Club (now Cabin Bluff) goes back a long way.

It all started in 1827 when the men of neighboring plantations got together for friendly hunting in an area of eastern Camden County south of the Great Satilla River. This was a forested tract abounding in game, especially wild turkeys. Two of the founding members were John Floyd and his son, Charles R. Floyd, both keenly involved in social and political affairs.

Members, said the bylaws, must meet and hunt together twice monthly; those who did not would be fined. There were other stringent rules, such as:

- Any member who shall fire at a deer at less than 40 yards and not kill it (when opportunity is fair) shall be fined at the discretion of the Club.
- A misfire of a member's gun due to lack of proper care and/or cleaning of the piece shall also be cause for a fine.
- Should disputes arise among members, the Club shall have the right to determine what is sportsmanlike and what is not. Should a member be judged guilty of unsportsmanlike conduct, he shall be subject to a fine.

It is not surprising that members who had repeated violations were stricken from the roster. To better check on members' activity, the secretary actually recorded the number of shots taken by each person, along with a tally of game killed. Fair game included deer, bear, wild boars, turkeys, gators, wild bulls, wildcats, and any of a wide variety of birds.

On one hunt in 1832 members slew four wild boars. On another, which took place on Independence Day 1838, the take was a boar, a wild bull, two turkeys, six does, and "three old bucks."

The club was highly social and gave many parties in which the entertainment was dugout canoe racing. Prizes ran as high as $10,000. On the party guest lists were members of several other coastal hunting and sporting clubs.

The Camden Club was discontinued during the Civil War. In the postwar years, parcels of the acreage were sold, mostly to commercial enterprises. Lumber became a big business and production of wood products and turpentine became vital to the region's economy.

In 1927 Howard Coffin, developer of Sea Island, wanted a recreational hideout for the guests at his new luxury resort. He bought the old hunting lands in Camden County, acquiring more than 60,000 acres from several different owners. He named it Sea Island Pasture and set about making it more attractive by restoring and expanding the old hunting lodge. There were other improvements, including new roads, phone lines, cottages, fire lanes, artesian wells, and better dock facilities. Coffin allowed a limited harvesting of timber products and also set up a forestry management program headquartered at Cabin Bluff.

In the lodge, before a great stone fireplace, Coffin would entertain his most distinguished guests, including explorers, authors, and political figures. Perhaps his most famous guests were President and Mrs. Calvin Coolidge.

In 1942, when the Sea Island Company sold the property to the Brunswick Pulp and Paper Company, a satellite of the Mead and Scott Paper enterprises, production of forest products accelerated. Much wood pulp was needed for paper-making and crews of laborers, caretakers, and forestry experts were employed. The lodge became an executive conference center, attracting industry officials from all over the world.

In the early 1990s the property is still a hunting reserve for employees and guests of the large paper-making concerns.

TWENTY-FOUR

ON THE LINE

When Telephone History Was Made

If it sounds amazing, it was! In the teens of the twentieth century, Georgia's Jekyll Island was part of an unfolding drama that included Alexander Graham Bell, the president of the United States, some naughty oyster shells, and an important businessman's sore ankle.

Here's what happened.

Early in 1915 Theodore N. Vail, first president of AT&T, was vacationing at the exclusive Jekyll Island Club. Because of a fall that injured his ankle, Vail was hobbling around and therefore unable to go to New York for the formal opening of a recently completed transcontinental telephone line. He fretted over his lameness as the scheduled date of January 25 approached.

Vail had plenty of clout, it seems. Immobilized, yet imperious, he ordered 1,000 miles of wire strung between New York and Jekyll so that he might participate in the historic event. Then he couldn't make up his mind about going north at the last minute, so all along the line there were hundreds of men awaiting his decision before they rigged the extra wire.

It was the culmination of what seemed incredible to the public. Chicago, reached from the East Coast in 1892, had long been regarded as the farthest frontier of transmitted speech. Then Denver was reached in 1911. Longer and longer distances became possible, leading to the great event of January 1915, when the starting point was the New York office of the phone company with speech directed to San Francisco.

The honored guest in New York was Alexander Graham Bell, inventor of the telephone. In the Washington group were President Woodrow Wilson and members of the National Geographic Society. In San Francisco, Thomas A. Watson, Bell's assistant in the development of the telephone, was the chief figure. At Jekyll Island, Theodore Vail, his ankle propped on a pillow, listened on his headset.

As a lead-in, Bell established contact with Watson. It was a historic moment and Bell used the exact words of his first transmitted sentence back in 1876, "Mr. Watson, come here. I want you." Watson replied, "It would take a week for me to do that now."

A bit later, it was announced that President Wilson, in Washington, was on the wire. He congratulated Dr. Bell first, then, told that Vail was on the line, he initiated a conversation that went like this:

"This is the President. I have just been speaking across the continent."

"Oh, yes."

"Before I give up the telephone I want to extend my congratulations to you on the consummation of this remarkable work."

"Thank you."

"I am very sorry to hear that you are sick."

"I am getting along nicely. I am sort of a cripple, that's all."

"I hope you will be well soon. Good-bye, Mr. Vail."

"Thank you. Good-bye, Mr. President."

A placid conversation, and surely nothing exciting or newsworthy. But as the president hung up, someone proposed three cheers for Mr. Vail. As the hurrahs dashed electronically across the country, it topped off what must have been magic moments for the AT&T president.

*In 1965, at a fiftieth anniversary celebration of the first
transcontinental phone call, a replica of the original
telephone was placed on the lawn near the Rockefeller
Cottage. It was erected by the Dixie Chapter, Telephone
Pioneers of America.* [Courtesy Jekyll Island Museum]

In Georgia, crews had worked overtime getting Vail's special wire from Savannah to Brunswick, then it was another headache getting it across the marshes to Jekyll. Checking to be sure the line was clear, they came upon a tree growing out of a drainage ditch. Water in the ditch had exposed the roots and it was so weakened by washed-out dirt that it threatened to fall and break the line. In desperation, the men tried to cut it down but, before they could do so a puff of wind caught the leaning tree and down it went—right across the line. The rupture was repaired by an emergency crew.

When crewmen arrived at Jekyll in a boat, bearing coils of cable, there was a comical situation. The island was so exclusive that they were refused landing permission. Vail had to be contacted before the necessary authorization was granted.

Two lines were strung to the island. The first lasted only a short time because oyster shells cut through the rubber insulation. Again, work crews labored feverishly and a second, lead-covered cable was strung.

In monetary terms, the San Francisco line soon paid for itself; but, even if it had not, it would have been a success because of the prestige it gave the Bell Company.

In January 1965 a fiftieth anniversary celebration commemorating that famous call was held at Jekyll Island. On hand were Gov. Carl Sanders and several phone company officials. A memorial, a pedestal supporting a replica of that original 1915 telephone, was placed on the lawn near the Rockefeller Cottage by the Dixie Chapter, Telephone Pioneers of America.

TWENTY-FIVE

BORDER SKIRMISH

It Looked Like War in 1894

In 1894, when the Brunswick Light Horse Guard, a unit of militia, was ordered to report to Waycross, the men thought a riot had occurred. Actually, it was more like mobilization for war, a display of armed might in which Georgia squared off against her sister state of Florida. And all because of a prizefight!

A boxing match had been scheduled in Jacksonville between British champion Charlie Mitchell and the popular James J. Corbett, who had gained the heavyweight title two years before by outlasting John L. Sullivan.

Corbett was not only a fine boxer but also something of a dude. An ex-bank clerk who liked to dress well, he was a clean-living, well-conditioned athlete who stood six feet one and fought at 184 pounds. The movie *Gentleman Jim* (1942), starring Errol Flynn, focused new attention on Corbett, who was smart, well-mannered, and as nimble-footed as a ballet dancer.

Once the fight was announced, however, there was public opposition. Gov. Henry Mitchell of Florida (no relation to the boxer) went public with, "We do not want this fight to take place in the Sunshine State!"

At that time there was heavy sentiment against the "ruffians of the ring" and the sport was largely condemned as

111

brutal and barbaric. Then, too, there was a question of the legality of such a contest under existing state laws.

The sheriff of Duval County in Florida was ordered to use force if necessary to halt the fisticuffs, and the governor took steps to mobilize state troops. All this to the dismay of loyal fight fans who wanted to see the battle take place. Meanwhile, Corbett and Mitchell ignored the hubbub as they set up training camps, and the advance betting, favoring Corbett, got underway.

Across the state line, Gov. William Northen was worried. He had heard that, due to ill feelings in Florida, the fight might be moved to Georgia. At once he became indignant and took steps to safeguard his home soil against this disgraceful exhibition.

Governor Northen wanted to protect his state from "invasion by half-naked men with fists for gold." He warmed up the state troops and called out several militia units. At Waycross, the main railroad junction in southeast Georgia, he made the statement, "Our best efforts will be put forth for the maintenance of law and the preservation of the public peace." He posted guards at the state line and gave orders to stop and search all northbound trains. It looked like war.

Waycross began to look like an armed camp. But folks weren't taking it too seriously. There was a sort of carnival atmosphere and the young ladies of the town were especially delighted to have the soldiers there. Friendships began to develop, causing a new problem: unhappy mothers of Waycross petitioned the governor to "remove the troops for the well-being of our daughters—or else!"

At the height of the tension some fifty miles of railroad leading into Georgia from Florida were being watched in case of an invasion, and spies were sent to Jacksonville to report on the movements of the two fighters. When rumors started that they were about to cross the St. Marys River, a horrified Governor Northen ordered a flotilla of fully armed small boats to patrol, watching all possible crossing places with vigilance.

Artist's conception of the big fight in Jacksonville in 1894. Mitchell (left) sports the British Union Jack emblem on his belt, while Corbett has a field of stars. Corbett won the fight in the third round.

About this time Corbett and Mitchell, amazed at the efforts to keep them out of Georgia, decided to remain in Jacksonville. Now the promoters went ahead and, despite continued public opposition, scheduled the battle for January 25, 1894.

At 2:30 P.M. at the old fairgrounds in Fairfield, the fight took place, witnessed by a crowd of 1,800. But it was an anticlimax after all the preliminary skirmishing; Corbett won an easy victory in the third round. Afterwards, both fighters were arrested, then each was released on $5,000 bond. Later they were acquitted of all charges.

So it was that the "War of '94" was over without a shot being fired. All the soldiers left Waycross, to the sorrow of the town's belles, and the other troops demobilized and went home. Rural Georgia returned to its peaceful ways.

Did things stay peaceful between Georgia and Florida? Well, almost. A kind of war still breaks out once a year, in the fall. Just ask the fans who go to the annual gridiron clash between the Florida Gators and the Georgia Bulldogs!

TWENTY-SIX

PROHIBITION

The Rum-runners and the Lawmen

Mother makes brandy from cherries,
Pa distills whiskey and gin;
Sister sells wine from the grapes on our vine—
Good grief, how the money rolls in!

The law was broken many times during Prohibition and lots of money changed hands. Whole families in Georgia, as in other parts, were in the illegal game, secretly making or importing the stuff and marketing it to turn over a profit. Lawmen often looked the other way, sometimes taking bribes to get in on the big splits of "hootch money."

Police in the coastal islands, finding it hard to locate moonshine stills at ground level, got smart and took to the air. Flying lightweight, slow planes, they would watch for a trickle of smoke coming from a deserted or swampy area. "There it is!" they would yell, then circle to land for an arrest. In just this way they closed down a number of stills, especially in Camden County.

Cumberland Island was a prime source of moonshine. An enterprising bootlegger set up business at Pine Island, separated by a creek from the main part of Cumberland.

As word got around, this place acquired a new name; people would ask, "What's going on over there?" and would be told, "Hush your mouth!" Pretty soon it became known as Hush-Your-Mouth Island.

Later, this same moonshiner opened a branch at Little Cumberland. His new still was soon doing more business than the first, as a constant stream of boats arrived from many coastal points. He even used the deserted light-house on Little Cumberland for part of his enterprise.

Distilleries in Camden County turned out corn whiskey, most of it made along the St. Marys River. The water there was just right, coming as it did out of cypress swamps and containing tannic acid. It was said to make a mighty tasty brand of liquor.

For a time, a father and his two sons were in the bootleg trade together in southern Camden, but persistent fed-erals finally nabbed them in an unorthodox manner. A couple of agents were flying over the area, following up a tip that the father and his sons were making corn light-ning down there, but they were unsure exactly where. As their plane passed overhead, the moonshiners, thinking it was a cash customer, waved at them from their boat dock, and those in the plane waved back. Now the law-men had them spotted, so they landed nearby and got a boat. Imagine the surprise of the whiskey-making trio when the two noncustomers tied up at their dock and made the arrest. All three ended up in jail.

Moonshining was one thing, but most of the illegal brew that entered Georgia during Prohibition was im-ported. Once the pipeline was set up, great quantities of liquid spirits flowed to the United States from Europe and the Caribbean. Scotch from Great Britain and rum from the islands were especially in demand, and a case of booze costing four or five dollars would bring one hundred dol-lars or more on the mainland. That was good money in those days.

Bimini, Nassau, or Havana were the intermediate stop-ping points and from there the stuff would be toted either

The sailing vessel Mary Langdon, *a rum-runner, after capture. It is flanked by two Coast Guard ships, the cutter* Redwing (left) *and the patrol boat CG-237* (right).

by boat or plane to the U.S. coast. Delivery vessels, designated "rum-runners," made good use of secret bays and inlets and would scoot over from the Bahamas, having many a merry chase with the Coast Guard. Occasionally, steamers and tankers would carry the booze and lay offshore, and smaller, faster boats would venture out to pick up the cargo. Once the liquor was landed, there were different ways of distributing it to a thirsty nation—plane, train, or automobile.

In the summer of 1928 an entire railroad car containing high-grade whiskey stood on a sidetrack behind the Oglethorpe Hotel in Brunswick. Police were almost fooled when, acting on a tip, they examined the boxcar's manifest, which declared its destination as New Jersey and its cargo as "crossarm planks." Upon examination they did find a few planks, but these merely camouflaged the real load, a vast amount of liquid spirits.

Much of the liquor that came into Florida by sea was sent north by highway. In March 1929 Glynn County lawmen noticed a "very unusual looking Studebaker coupe" going up State Route 17, so they gave chase and stopped it. What aroused their suspicion was a deep bottom. There was a compartment under the body, extending almost the entire length of the car. There were also extra springs to handle heavy loads. A search revealed about three dozen cases of William Penn rye whiskey. The driver was jailed.

Prohibition brought out some rare characters, many of them salty, adventurous soldiers of fortune. One of the most successful was Duke Crossman, an airplane pilot who made plenty of money carrying liquor into St. Simons Island from such points as Nassau, Bimini, and St. Augustine. Duke was a stubborn, "I'll do it or else!" fellow who seems to have never failed to bring home the goodies, eluding the lawmen every time.

One time Duke was coming in with a heavy load, all the cargo compartments in his two-seater, open cockpit plane being stuffed with liquor. As he approached Redfern Field, a small airport located (in the 1920s) where a couple of shopping centers can be found today, he noticed that the boys on the ground were signaling him *not* to land! To Duke this meant only one thing: the revenue agents were down there. Turning, he flew to Jekyll and unloaded his cargo on a deserted beach. When he came back to Redfern Field, the authorities searched him to no avail. He waited until they were gone and then went back to Jekyll for his loot.

In another similar episode, Cap. Albert Brockington, an old-time Brunswick harbor pilot, had a strange encounter with a rum-runner. As he was returning from a rendezvous with a large steamer just offshore, he noticed an SOS signal flashing from a dim, hand-held light. A small boat had gone aground with heavy seas pounding it and was in danger of breaking up. Brockington threw a line to the two men on the small boat and was soon able to pull it free. As he towed the boat toward the docks, to his surprise the men on the rescued craft cut the line and disappeared. Later, in talking over the incident, Brockington and his cohorts decided they were rummys who did not want to be landed where he was taking them.

Probably no character of the Prohibition era was more colorful than Big Bill McCoy, a rangy man with a booming voice and shoulders like a bull. He captained a couple of sailing vessels, and to the authorities he was known as a slippery rummy who could never be caught.

In the early 1920s Big Bill was in Nassau with his first schooner, the *Henry L. Marshall,* when a buddy who also smuggled illegal spirits asked him if he'd like to take 1,500 cases of liquor to Georgia at ten dollars a case. Big Bill jumped at the chance.

So it was that McCoy made preparations to sail to St. Catherine's Sound, just south of Savannah. His buddy went ahead, taking a seaplane and promising to have cargo lighters available for unloading. All went well as the *Marshall,* with its heavy load, reached the Georgia coast and made contact with the barges, as promised.

Night was falling when Bill, his partner in crime, and the rest of his crew began to unship the 1,500 cases of spirits. This was a long process and halfway through, McCoy saw the lights of a large ship outside the harbor, which he recognized as a Coast Guard cutter on patrol. With the *Marshall* blacked out, the men waited tensely, but they were not observed.

Away went the lighters, just before daylight, all loaded up. Only 100 cases remained on the *Marshall,* and this was a bonus that Bill was saving for a friend in Nassau. He decided to turn in, being exhausted. Just as he did so a crewman, in great alarm, called him back up to the deck. On the sound, a short distance away, two seaplanes had landed and now swung at their moorings. Bill could see the insignia of the U.S. Coast Guard.

"All hands on deck," he ordered. "Dump the rest of the liquor overboard."

The men formed a line and did as they were told, passing the remaining 100 cases out of the hold and into the drink, to the sorrow of some of the men, "Aw captain, we're throwing away the makings of a pub," said one. To ease his distress, this fellow knocked the neck off a bottle and fortified himself as he worked.

In the full light of day, McCoy noticed that the two seaplanes were deserted. Later, crews returned, throttled up, and took off with a roar. Bill concluded that stormy weather had driven them off their course and they had landed there to find some gasoline. As they faded from sight, he cursed in frustration for having jettisoned all that whiskey.

Big Bill McCoy went on to other successes as a rumrunner, eluding the Coast Guard many times and amassing a fortune of more than $200,000. Eventually, however, the law of averages caught up with him and he was captured by a Coast Guard gunboat and towed to New York harbor. After serving a brief jail term (and paying hefty legal fees), he went back to his old boat-building business at Daytona Beach.

Looking back, it's generally conceded that Prohibition was a failure. It was obvious the law could never be totally enforced and, indeed, so many people were doing illegal things that a wide-scale disrespect for legal standards grew. Some say this disrespect has carried over to the present time.

In the 1930s, humorist Franklin P. Adams looked back at the dry era with a poem:

It's left a trail of graft and slime.
It's filled our land with vice and crime;
It don't prohibit worth a dime.
It just can't stop what it's meant to stop;
Oh, Prohibition is an awful flop!

BLOODY BATTLES

(Top) *A restored Fort King George, completed in 1988,
has proved popular with tourists and re-enactors alike.*
(Bottom) *At restored Fort King George near Darien, various costume dramas and re-enactments are held
each year.* [Courtesy Georgia Department of Natural
Resources]

TWENTY-SEVEN

COLONIAL STRONGHOLDS

Forts along the Coast

For the soldiers at Fort Argyle on the Ogeechee River, it must have been a Maytag repairman's existence: no action at all.

That's true of many of those old colonial forts along the Georgia coast. They served as valuable communication links but there was little diversion to liven the monotony.

Action or not, many of the forts have now returned to the soil, but others remain, perhaps in replica form, and they provide a fascinating opportunity for moderns to understand and appreciate the heritage of the Golden Isles.

Let's look back over 250 years at some of the outposts that guarded the coastline. Let's see what motivation created them in the first place and what circumstances caused their downfall and/or deterioration.

Ringing the city of Savannah were a number of small batteries, but these were not major forts, for most of them had but a few cannon and limited armament and personnel. They were designed to provide a defensive screen to protect the town from minor raids. A few of these were Thunderbolt and Skidaway to the southeast, Sterling's Fort to the southwest, and Abercorn and Ebenezer to the northwest. Soldiers and their families farmed small land grants to form tiny fortified villages, which contributed little to the total defense of the area.

Fort Argyle was also a part of the defense network for Savannah, lying southwest of the city on the west bank of the Ogeechee. James Oglethorpe laid it out in 1733 and named it Fort Argyle for John Campbell, the Duke of Argyle. Square shaped, 110 feet to a side, it had a prominent moat around it. The dirt excavated for the moat was piled within for an earthen wall, or curtain. There were about a dozen huts inside, and all around the structure was a fence, or palisade, of stout logs.

The brief history of this fort shows no military action, only a couple of bloody murders. In 1740 troops were returning after a foray when they found the bodies of two servants, minus their heads, floating in the nearby river. An Indian alarm went out, but it was quickly realized that no Indian had committed the crime. Scalping was the preferred Indian method, not beheading. A bit later, two escaped prisoners, a Spanish doctor and an Irishman, confessed to the murders. Both were executed.

Fort Argyle was one of the weaker fortifications and not really strategic in the colony's defense. In 1747 it was vacated and a few years later was rapidly falling apart. No trace remains of this old military post today.

As forts went up in Georgia, it was a great relief to the folks in the Carolinas, for now there was added protection against the Spanish, down in Florida. One of these outposts that made them breathe more easily was Fort King George near the mouth of the Altamaha River in McIntosh County.

The British picked a man named John ("Tuscarora Jack") Barnwell to build the fort and he seems to have been the perfect choice. In July 1721 he sailed down from Charleston with a party of scouts, Indian helpers, and "sawyers" (carpenters).

Somehow, in spite of heat, mosquitoes, and the threat of attack from hostile tribesmen and the Spanish, they got the work done, fashioning a blockhouse, barracks building, and several thatched huts. The striking blockhouse was three stories high and twenty-six feet square at the base; it seemed a bit top-heavy until one considered that the third floor, overlooking the lower walls, would serve as a lookout station.

Fort King George was not a healthy place. When it was garrisoned in 1722, the men suffered from fevers and malnutrition; diseases took their toll and Indian raids added to the casualty list. In winter, the occupants suffered bitterly from the cold. Finally, British authorities decided to close the place down, and the fort was evacuated in 1727.

Modern visitors can enjoy a restored Fort King George. Completed in the fall of 1988, it is an exact replica of the original.

Gen. James Oglethorpe built Fort Frederica in 1736 on St. Simons Island as additional protection against the Spanish. Its location was the west side of the island, on the Frederica River. Oglethorpe laid out a town adjacent to it, also called Frederica.

In order to properly garrison and defend this settlement, Oglethorpe went to England to raise a regiment of light infantry. Besides these British regulars, a number of provincial units were quartered there from time to time.

Fort Frederica was large, roughly square-shaped, with a regular bastion at each corner and a sort of spur battery jutting out beyond the walls on the river side. There were sod-faced earthen walls and a long row of palisades planted in a moat. These fortifications surrounded a storehouse, powder magazine, well, and blacksmith shop. The town had houses of log, frame, brick, and tabby (a local building material made of lime and shells).

In 1742 hostilities with the Spanish ended and Oglethorpe's forces were largely disbanded. As the military involvement ended, the economy collapsed; the fort gradually fell into disrepair and Frederica became a declining community. Nowadays, only portions of the fort and barracks remain, along with foundation elements of the town, yet these are prominent as tourist attractions.

Fort St. Simons was the British bastion of protection at the southern end of St. Simons Island. It, too, was a large, square, earthen-walled fortification, containing seven cannon trained outward to control the harbor entrance. Modern visitors to the island museum and lighthouse walk in approximately the same location.

Along the beach toward the east direction was Delegal's Fort, a tabby blockhouse surrounded by a horseshoe-shaped earthen wall. Between the two forts was another battery, and nearby were several clapboard huts serving as barracks for the soldiers and living quarters for their families.

The British kept three or four companies of infantry in these fortifications to safeguard the southern approaches, but these strongholds were abandoned to the Spanish during their invasion so that troop strength could be concentrated at Fort Frederica.

The Spaniards destroyed most of Fort St. Simons when they withdrew. Here, again, with no more battles looming, the fort and its adjacent batteries fell into neglect. There is no sign remaining of these fortifications today.

Fort St. Andrews and Fort Prince William were outposts built on Cumberland Island as further protection against the Spanish.

Oglethorpe wanted a lookout fort at the north end of Cumberland and he laid out a stockade at the northwest tip, commanding the nearby waterways. This was Fort St. Andrews; although small, it was well positioned on a fifty-foot promontory.

At the southwest tip of the island he ordered a stronger, more strategic fort, to be called Fort Prince William. This would command the entrance to Amelia Channel, the St. Marys River, and all the inland approaches to both Jekyll and St. Simons islands.

These two forts were useful in the repulse of the Spaniards in 1742, when both saw quite a bit of action. Later, there seems to have been no threat of outside invasion and the forts rapidly fell into disrepair. Efforts in modern times to find evidence of their exact locations have largely failed; all traces have been covered by the dust of time.

TWENTY-EIGHT

THE WAR OF JENKINS' EAR

Battle or Brouhaha?

Robert Jenkins was a humble British subject trying to make a living as a smuggler. Little did he know that when the Spanish sliced off his ear it would cause a rumble of international hostilities.

In 1739 Jenkins testified in the House of Commons how the Spanish had boarded his privateer brig off the Florida coast in search of contraband. Finding nothing, one of the officers in his wrath had drawn a sword and cut off one of Jenkins's ears. To prove it, Jenkins displayed the earless side of his head, while the members of Parliament bristled in indignation. As further evidence, the smuggler held up the grisly relic itself, carefully wrapped in cotton.

The fact that the ear had been removed several years earlier did not alter the British resolve to retaliate. Soon after, war broke out between the two nations, and it was said that one of the factors causing it was the inhuman treatment of Mr. Jenkins. The series of eighteenth-century hostilities between England and Spain is now called the War of the Austrian Succession (1740–1748) and the Seven Years' War (1756–1763). The British colonials in America used the term the French and Indian

Wars, but the English called the opening conflict the War of Jenkins' Ear.

One of the most enthusiastic promoters of war with Spain was Capt. Edward Vernon, a Royal Navy officer and also a member of Parliament. Vernon said, "Give me six ships and I will capture the Spanish fortress and treasure warehouse at Porto Bello on the Panama Coast." The navy gave him the ships and promoted him to admiral, and he accomplished the job in November 1739.

Vernon wasn't the sort to rest on his laurels. He made more raids on the Spaniards, frequently recruiting extra personnel from the American colonies. Among those who served under Vernon was a young captain from Virginia named Lawrence Washington. After the war he established a plantation overlooking the Potomac and named it after his commanding officer. Later, Mount Vernon passed into the hands of his younger brother, George, and as the home of our first president became a national historical treasure.

The English wars of the eighteenth century, against a series of European adversaries, were primarily inspired by the growing world economy, command of the seas, and control of colonies, both in India and in the New World. Much of the American action in the War of Jenkins' Ear in the American colonies centered in Georgia where the British and Spanish disputed the Georgia-Florida boundary.

In 1739 Gen. James Oglethorpe of Britain tried to capture Florida but failed. In 1742 his troops defeated the Spanish at the battle of Bloody Marsh on St. Simons Island. This ended the War of Jenkins' Ear in America but the conflict continued in Europe.

One happy fellow didn't care how long it lasted. One-eared Robert Jenkins was basking in a tropical paradise; as compensation for his misfortune, he had been named supervisor of the British East India Company's office on St. Helena in the South Atlantic. Here, enjoying his ample salary, he was far away from worldly cares and glad to be done with the smuggling business.

Then some facts came out which clouded his integrity. According to Florida historians Cabell and Hanna, the shocking "evidence" he had shown Parliament was no ear at all, merely a bit of dried-up rabbit skin. It also came out that the actual ear had been separated from his head while he was in a pillory stock, a colonial punishment in which wrongdoers were locked in place for public display.

Jenkins, when confronted with accusations about the true tale of his amputation, would reply "How dare they question me?"

TWENTY-NINE

BLOODY MARSH

A Vital Chapter in Our History

Don Manuel de Montiano, governor of Spanish Florida, was a cautious man. In 1742, after his disastrous defeat at St. Simons Island, he sent a letter to his king. In language slanted to cast his forces in the most favorable light, he said, in part:

> I sent a rather small force northward from Fort St. Simons. While examining the road that leads to Fort Frederica, this force was attacked by a body of English and Indians in a narrow defile of the woods. Disorder followed.

That's putting it mildly.

The truth is the Spanish fled in plenty of disorder, and the British pursued in a long, running battle that led to the major engagement at Bloody Marsh. What happened there on July 7, 1742, was a turning point in southeastern military history.

Governor Montiano lost an opportunity that, by all odds, he should have won. His huge command, about 5,000 Spanish troops, was repulsed by a force of some 650 British, provincials, and Indians. Montiano concluded his report to the king by blaming five factors: the terrain was unfamiliar to his troops and highly overgrown with im-

131

penetrable undergrowth; few supplies; loss of thirteen ships of his original fleet in a furious storm; suspicion that the British, under Gen. James Oglethorpe, would get heavy reinforcements, and he had seen a few distant ships which convinced him the reinforcements were coming; and, lack of absolute surety of a successful withdrawal of his forces.

In contrast to the less-than-triumphant report of Governor Montiano, let's consider the British view, which has become the standard historical account.

Oglethorpe had advance warning of the Spanish approach. For a better tactical advantage he evacuated Fort St. Simons, a small stronghold at the southern tip of the island, and moved his entire garrison to Fort Frederica, about four miles to the north on the Frederica River. As the men lined up for inspection, their diversity was apparent: one company of British regulars; a unit of Scottish Highlanders from Darien with their traditional caps and tartans; a body of provincials, including colonial marines and rangers; and Indian allies, Yamacraws, Creeks, and Chickasaws.

The Spanish landed and took over the deserted Fort St. Simons. Their large force consisted of a regiment of artillery, one of dismounted dragoons, and one each of blacks and mulattos. There were also a few Cuban troops from Havana.

On July 7 a portion of this army marched northward through the woods. When within one mile of Fort Frederica they were attacked in what is called the Battle of Gully Hole Creek, this being the engagement mentioned by Montiano where there was "disorder." The fiery Oglethorpe, old records claim, was so eager to engage the Spanish that he couldn't wait for the Forty-second Regiment (British Regulars) to assemble, instead he leaped on a horse and led a mixed array of Highlanders, rangers, and Indians into a pitched battle that terrified the Spanish troops. In this encounter Oglethorpe dismounted and captured two of the enemy himself, thus inspiring his

Scottish Highlanders from Darien in period dress, posing just outside Fort King George in a re-enactment. The Highlanders gave General Oglethorpe a powerful assist at the Battle of Bloody Marsh. [Courtesy Georgia Department of Natural Resources]

men with a fine example of action by a field commander.

The retreating Spanish fled along the old Military Road, with Oglethorpe's forces in hot pursuit, sniping at the enemy all the way. When the English reached a broad marsh, Oglethorpe positioned a number of his units in an ambush position to be ready for the major advance by the enemy that was sure to take place. Then he went back to Frederica to assemble the rest of his army.

Meanwhile, when Montiano heard the news from men who came staggering into Fort St. Simons, he immediately issued marching orders to a larger body of his troops.

Thus the scene was set for a new engagement. The Spaniards came under attack at a marshy plateau on the eastern side of the island a few miles south of Fort Frederica. This encounter was severe enough to cause some of the British regulars to panic and hastily depart, soon followed by more troops.

It was then that Oglethorpe, hearing the distant firing, once again spurred his horse to a gallop and ordered the remaining troops at the fort to "Follow me!" In a short time he ran into some of his retreating soldiers and ordered them to turn around and rejoin the fray. Still hearing a sound of firing (and being sure some of the sounds were British guns), he inspired most of them to go back.

Meanwhile a contingent of colonial rangers and Highlanders at the rear of the retreat decided they would stand their ground. They regrouped and once again hid themselves in the bushes to await the Spanish advance.

They didn't have long to wait, for the enemy reinforcements soon came up the trail. One report says that the Spanish, observing the footprints of the English in rapid retreat, became overconfident, thinking the fighting was over for the day. They stacked their arms and began to prepare for lunch. At this point the palmettos erupted in fire and the Spanish were totally devastated. The defeat of the Spaniards was complete, and since then this stretch of ground, because of its gory heritage, has been called "Bloody Marsh."

Oglethorpe was elated to find that some of his platoons had held and the enemy had been routed. He followed the Spanish to within a mile or so of their camp, then went back to the fort to await developments. About this time he decided to try a night attack on the enemy, but this was not successful.

Then Oglethorpe ventured on a clever bit of strategy. He fashioned a fake letter, which he allowed to get into the hands of the Spanish commander. This message led the enemy to believe that Oglethorpe's forces were stronger than they really were and that he was about to be re-inforced by more ships and men from Charleston.

There was dissension in the Spanish ranks, and that letter filled them with added fear and indecision. At last concluding a council of war, they decided it was best to pull out and go back to St. Augustine. Montiano wrote his report explaining the whole unpleasant situation to his king.

The victory for the British was a decisive one, for if the Spanish had been able to gobble up Georgia, then move into the Carolinas, they might have had a tremendous hold on the East Coast. When they were repulsed, however, it saved these southern portions of the colonies for England.

THIRTY

HARE AND HOUNDS
Civil War Naval Chases

During the Civil War, Union warships played hare and hounds with Confederate blockade runners off the Georgia coast.

On April 19, 1861, within a week of the storming of Fort Sumter, President Lincoln ordered a blockade of Southern ports. At first it was ineffective, but as time went on Yankee blockaders began to put on the squeeze, especially around such ports as Savannah, Charleston, South Carolina, and Wilmington, North Carolina. They had to be vigilant because more and more blockade runners were sneaking in with clothing, food, medicine, and the urgently needed munitions of war; and they slipped away with tobacco, rice, and huge loads of cotton to be sold overseas to help the Confederacy finance the hostilities.

The most effective runners were altered steamers, such as riverboats. A sidewheeler would have her freeboard cut down until she had a low, rakish look. Fitted with a more powerful engine and a collapsible smokestack, she would be hard to spot and, indeed, many of these "gray ghosts of the sea" got through the blockade.

The Federal ships were also effective along the Georgia coast. They bottled up Savannah and Brunswick, the two best harbors, and placed a number of guardian vessels *inside* coastal inlets and sounds. For the men on these

The USS Alabama, *a three-masted sidewheeler, was one of the "sentry" ships stationed in the bays and inlets along the southern coast. For a time, she was stationed at St. Simons Sound. The* Alabama *took part in the capture of Fort Clinch at Fernandina, Florida, in March 1862.*

sentinel ships it was lonely duty, but the larger runners found the coast hard to penetrate for this reason. Smaller sailing ships did get through, from time to time.

In December 1861 the Yankee gunboat *Alabama* (not to be confused with the Confederate raider of the same name) trapped a schooner off Cumberland Island. It was a blockade runner loaded with smuggled goods and the *Alabama* ran the ship ashore. Hastily, unloading began and men could be seen carrying things off the sailing ship; but when the *Alabama* fired a warning shot the workers on the beach dropped everything and ran. The ship was easily captured. The valuable cargo—partially burned—included fruit, cigars, and shoes galore.

Skipper of the *Alabama* was Capt. Lewis West, a Bostonian, who seems to have had a lively sense of humor. He left a journal detailing his adventures in blockade duty and reported that the "seegars" were mighty good and he gave each of his crewmen a pair of the shoes.

In February 1862 Gen. Robert E. Lee ordered the military evacuation of the entire Brunswick area, including the islands. Lee felt that Savannah was the key to the South's military operations and all available troops and guns should be sent there without hesitation. Accordingly, Confederate forces withdrew from the Brunswick area and the Union was in complete control. As a parting shot, the rebels destroyed the St. Simons lighthouse so their enemies could not make use of it.

Again, Captain West and the sidewheeler *Alabama* enter the picture. In April, while on patrol at Jekyll Island, West went ashore to check on an abandoned earthwork gun battery. (This was on the west side of the island, just south of the present-day airport.) In his journal, he described the battery as a "perfect masterpiece of engineering," with earthworks thrown up on the sides and roof. Before leaving, he ordered the supporting timbers burned, thus caving in the roof and rendering the fort useless.

At St. Simons, West took a squad on a night march, having been instructed to "look for 20 rebels hiding on the island." This was dangerous duty, as they might be mistaken for rebels themselves and fired upon by fellow Yankees in the area. Later, the captain described the action: "We commenced plunging through the woods, thickets, and swamps, disturbing sundry rattlesnakes and alligators but not finding what we sought. The only trophies of the expedition were two 'secession cats' picked up by the men on the road, which were really valuable, as our old cat died about two months ago and rats have been abounding ever since."

Later in the war West assumed command of the USS *Fernandina*, a bark, which he called a "worn-out sailing vessel, unfit for duty." He was ordered to perform dull and tedious guard duty in St. Catherine's Sound, south of Savannah, a bay so shallow that it could only be used by smaller sailing ships. West's ship had to be towed to her anchorage at high tide and was unable to get back to sea. West lamented, "We have not room to move about and

Fort Clinch, at Fernandina, Florida (Amelia Island) was an early Union Navy objective. It was captured on March 3, 1862. [From Frank Leslie's Illustrated Newspaper]

nothing to do but wander about islands full of snakes and alligators."

Things may have been dull for Captain West, but for the blockader USS *Stettin* there was excitement on September 23, 1863. She was on afternoon patrol near St. Simons Island when suddenly lookouts spotted an approaching craft coming up fast from the north. The cry of "Black Snake!" went up from the decks of the *Stettin*, meaning the quarry had been sighted: a blockade runner.

It was the *Diamond*, a narrow sidewheeler with plenty of horsepower and a draft of only six feet. She had tried to enter Doboy Sound at Sapelo Island, but failing that, had passed the outer buoy at St. Simons, hoping to get into the channel. On board were liquors, shoes, boots, cigars, medicines, dry goods, and cutlery—items urgently needed by the war-torn South after three years of war.

Closing in with its objective at top speed, the *Stettin* fired a warning shot. At this, the *Diamond*, which had flown no colors at first, hoisted the British Union Jack, apparently thinking this might save them from capture.

Then came a warning salvo, along with the barked command, "Drop your anchor!" The *Diamond,* knowing the game was up, dropped her hook immediately.

A boat was lowered from the blockader and her captain and some officers rowed over to inspect the trophy. They were delighted at the cargo, because all crewmen and officers received a portion of the "swag" (money) when it was sold! A prize crew was set up and placed aboard the *Diamond,* with instructions to sail her to Philadelphia.

Meanwhile there were three forts guarding Savannah and all of them suffered bombardment. Fort Pulaski was taken by the Federals in April 1862, giving them command of the Savannah River, the harbor entrance to the port. Fort Jackson, on the river above the city, was captured in December 1864. That same month Gen. William T. Sherman's infantry finally forced the surrender of Fort McAllister on the Ogeechee River, which had guarded the back door to Savannah.

The Georgia coast again saw a flurry of action after the war, *long* after! In the spring of 1989 a Hollywood company filmed a Civil War battle scene on the beach at Jekyll Island. Part of the movie *Glory,* the action recreated the September 1863 storming of Battery Wagner at Charleston. There were no casualties, but those who saw the movie will agree, the fighting was fierce.

THIRTY-ONE

PELOT'S PRIZE
The Capture of the *Water Witch*

Lieutenant Tom Pelot was more than bored. He was itching for action.

All around him the Civil War was raging and here he was, wasting his days in peaceful guard duty at Savannah. All there was to do on his ship, the ironclad CSS *Georgia,* which he called the "mud tub," was check the ammunition and keep the decks clean. A wretched existence for an officer of spirit and ambition!

The boredom in Savannah wasn't the only reason the young lieutenant was frustrated. One of his tasks on the *Georgia* had been to persuade crewmen to reenlist when their terms expired. He was only partially successful, prompting a senior officer to remark that an "experienced and intelligent officer" might have had better luck. This made him yearn for combat even more.

Pelot was popular with the ladies, however. While living with the family of Captain Hanleiter, he was described by one of the captain's daughters as being charming, with graceful manners, and "handsome and [with] most military bearing." Wishing the young officer success, another daughter had pinned a Cape jasmine blossom on his coat.

As he paced the decks of the lonely mud tub, Pelot decided he wouldn't wait for action, he would make some. He came up with a daring plan: in nearby Ossabaw Sound a

Yankee warship, the *Water Witch*, was anchored and he was sure it could be taken by a determined band. Immediately, he went to his superior officers and sold the plan. For the mission, he was assigned 115 crewmen and 15 officers, while for transportation he was allowed seven cotton barges.

The *Water Witch* was one of several Union patrol vessels stationed at intervals inside bays and inlets along the coast. Supplementary to the blockading ships, they watched for small, fast rebel blockade runners sneaking in and out with supplies and ammunition. The *Water Witch* was a two-masted sidewheeler, 150 feet long, a sharp-looking gunboat that had served with the Gulf Blockading Squadron at the mouth of the Mississippi. Now she was stationed in Ossabaw Sound at the outlet of the Ogeechee River. In command was Lt. Comdr. Austin Pendergrast.

For most of these sentinel ships, life was just as dull as it was for the Confederate sailors on harbor duty. By late spring 1864, the ship had been on guard for many months. Crewmen, with little to relieve their monotony, were restless and quarrelsome, while her officers, probably feeling that the ship was well armed, were lulled into a false sense of security. The time was right for a sneak attack.

Pelot's makeshift fleet left Savannah on May 31, 1864. The men's morale was high, being in Pelot's words "ready for a brush" as they rowed down the Vernon River, a tributary, toward their destination. The next day, June 1, they arrived at a small rebel stronghold called Fortress Beaulieu. To Pelot's disappointment, the commandant told him "the bird had flown," meaning the *Water Witch* had shifted its position to St. Catherine's Sound to the south.

Pelot stationed scouts at a lookout point near Ossabaw, and the following day the men reported that the ship was back in her old place. Once again, on the evening of June 2, the flotilla cast off, rowing with muffled oars. The mood of the band was still positive, although the night had turned stormy and there were rain squalls and occasional flashes of lightning.

The Water Witch *was a two-masted sidewheeler 150 feet long mounting four guns with a complement of ninety men. She was stationed in Ossabaw Sound when captured by rebel forces.*

As they neared their quarry, Pelot displayed a brand of leadership that no doubt inspired his followers to extra efforts. Standing up in the lead boat, he called out: "Now, men, the hour has come. The eyes of your country are on you! Mark well what record you leave to history tonight."

Now, with each burst of lightning the men strained forward to see, and suddenly there it was: the towering black hull of an anchored ship. At this point they divided into two groups, some boats going to the right side, some to the left.

In securing the *Water Witch*, Pendergrast had followed his usual routine. The crew was inspected at quarters, fires were banked, and ammunition was brought up for guns. The deck watch was posted, and soon all was quiet as the crew retired for the night. Then, at 2:00 A.M. a strange craft was sighted, followed by others perhaps forty yards away. Came the hail, "Boats ahoy! Who goes there?"

"Runaway Negroes," yelled one fellow from the boats.

This was ruse, a bit of deception calculated to fool the enemy and put them off their guard. But Pelot's sense of honor would not allow this. "We are rebels," he shouted. "Give way, boys. Three cheers and board her!"

The alarm was sounded on the steamer, causing a flurry of activity. Below decks, officers and men, most groggy with sleep, struggled to find clothes and sidearms. Captain Pendergrast, half-dressed, rushed to the deck and called out, "All hands, repel boarders. Slip the chain and start the engine." A hail of bullets sprayed the barges, causing several casualties.

Each of the Confederate barges was equipped with ladders and grappling irons and as they bumped against the hull of the gunboat, the men worked feverishly to get them into position. At this point they encountered a serious obstruction. When they started to clamber aboard the Union vessel, they were stopped by protective netting. They began hacking away, and some managed to climb over it. All this time, guns were blazing away and though they returned the fire as best they could, it was here that they suffered most of their casualties. Some of the most deadly fire came from a crewman who was in charge of the small-arms rack. Standing his ground, he fired again and again until he fell with several bullets in him.

One of the first to reach the deck was Lieutenant Pelot. Unfortunately, he was observed by one of the defenders during a flash of lightning and was shot through the heart.

In the hand-to-hand fighting, cutlasses, sabers, and pikes were used, but the advantage was clearly on the side of the Confederates, thanks to the element of surprise. At one point a member of the boarding party, armed with a cutlass, rushed to an open hatch door and yelled, "Stay down there or I'll cut your damn noses off!" No one came up. In fact, a later report indicated that many in the

Yankee crew showed no desire to resist. "They seemed paralyzed with fear," said the report.

Captain Pendergrast, although putting up a good fight, was subdued in a cutlass duel. After suffering a head wound, he was knocked through an open hatch and tumbled down the ladder. Lying there, unable to get up, he muttered, "I surrender."

In twenty minutes the ship was in the hands of the rebels. Lieutenant Joseph Price, second in command, had taken charge after Pelot's death. He found that six in his raiding force had been killed, thirteen wounded. One of his first orders of business was to get his men some food, as they had had little in the past three days, and supplies were plentiful aboard the *Water Witch*.

Fearing a counterattack, Price, his head swathed in bandages, then began to get their prize to Savannah. The ship could not sail the ocean route because of the blockade, so the only solution was to float her to the city by way of the inland waterways. This was a delicate maneuver because there was much shoal water, and, sure enough, the ship soon ran aground.

News of the capture caused much excitement throughout the South. In Savannah especially, there was jubilation, for there had been little to cheer about lately. The heroic Lieutenant Pelot was given a grand funeral and was buried at Laurel Grove Cemetery. Captain Pendergrast, on the other hand, was later given a Federal court-martial for allowing his ship to be captured.

The rest of the story is anticlimatic. The *Water Witch* was refloated once her armament and supplies were unshipped; but later, while working her way through the Vernon River route, she was hopelessly snagged a narrow stream and could be maneuvered no farther. They talked of cutting off a portion of the shoreline to form a passage, but nothing came of it.

Then came the final chapter. When Gen. Sherman's Union troops approached Savannah in later 1864, the *Water Witch* was burned to keep her from being recaptured.

THIRTY-TWO

WORLD WAR II

Terror in the Atlantic

Coastal Georgians knew about World War II; they had been reading the papers, their sons had gone off to war, and there was rationing of some consumer goods. Then, in April 1942, the war hit home with fearful reality.

At 2:00 A.M. on April 8, 1942, two medium-sized U.S. tankers were torpedoed by a German submarine off Brunswick, and twenty-two crewmen perished. The two ships, the *Esso Baton Rouge* and the *Oklahoma,* were thirteen miles off the coast and were struck fifty minutes apart. Survivors were rescued by the Coast Guard.

As lifeboats were pulling away, the Nazi sub came to the surface and shelled the first stricken tanker, leaving it a flaming hulk. There was no shelling of the second tanker, nor was there any attempt to shoot at the lifeboats.

In Brunswick, the injured were taken to hospitals and local citizens provided clothes for some of the rest, who sorely needed them. After the survivors were interviewed by reporters, they were given hotel accommodations and arrangements were made to get them back home. These men had high praise for the kindness of the Georgians. When asked how they felt about the war, every one said he wanted to go to sea again.

The sub attacks, so close to home, had a frightening

Nazi U-boats took a heavy toll of allied tankers in the early days of World War II. Here a tanker buckles amidships after a torpedo attack.

effect. Plane spotters became more vigilant, underground shelters were built, and people became much more aware of the war.

In Jesup there was a rumor that Brunswick had been invaded by the Germans. Quickly, the Jesup militia was assembled at the American Legion Hall where M-1 rifles and boots were issued. When the truth came out (no invasion after all), the alert was canceled before the boys started for the coast.

Plenty of tankers were hit during those early months of the war and it's tragic, looking back, that commercial interests actually helped the German subs. Resorts and hotels refused to black out or even dim their lights. The bright glow could be seen far out to sea and American ships, hugging the coast, were silhouetted, making perfect targets for sub captains looking through their periscopes. Not until May 18, 1942, was a stringent dim-out enforced, but by that time many ships had gone to the bottom, with many lives lost.

At first, this sub-tanker warfare was pitifully one sided. Effective radar and sonar had not yet been developed and the cargo ships had only small, inadequate armament. The U-boat captains became more confident, attacking in broad daylight with no fear of surfacing to shell the tankers. Early in the war the Nazis were launching one sub per day, but records show only a few of them were sunk in this period.

In contrast, hundreds of tankers were picked off as they skirted the coastline. In the worst month, May 1942, (when the dim-out was finally enforced), some eighty-six tankers were sunk.

In 1987 a German book, *Axis Submarine Successes: 1939–1945,* gave complete statistics on all the Fatherland's U-boat kills. It verified that the tankers hit off Brunswick were the victims of *U-123,* commanded by Kapitaenleutnant Hardegen, who had sunk eight ships and damaged several others during his coastal raids. This officer received the Knight's Cross with Oak Leaves for his successes.

It's interesting that one of the tankers, the *Esso Baton Rouge,* was salvaged and repaired in Brunswick. Back at sea, while making an Atlantic crossing in 1943, she was hit again and sunk.

By the summer of 1943 a big change came about in antisubmarine warfare. Thanks to better U.S. detection equipment, the U-boats were the ones suffering the big losses, not the Allied ships.

During the dreadful early months, St. Simons Island came into the limelight when it was mentioned on a national news program. In May 1942 the broadcaster Walter Winchell badmouthed the hotels and tourist shops for not paying attention to the dim-out. He urged the merchants on the island to "shape up." And they did.

THIRTY-THREE

OLD-FASHIONED HONOR

Dueling under the Oaks

Way back in the 1700s dueling came to Georgia, along with other Old World customs. Men settled their "affairs of honor" at the point of a sword or with a brace of dueling pistols.

One of the first duels in the new colony took place on St. Simons Island in 1741. The location of this gruesome contest was just outside the recently built Fort Frederica. On May 10, 1741, several of Gen. James Oglethorpe's officers were dining in the barracks and wine was flowing freely. A dispute arose between Capt. Richard Norbury and Capt. Albert Desbrisay. Records do not show the cause of the fracas (a woman?), but fellow officers stepped in and cooled them down. After a few more toasts the party broke up and the men left the barracks.

But when the two belligerents met on the grounds outside, a brand new argument erupted. Tempers flared and it could only be solved by combat, so the two drew their swords and went at it. The others tried to stop them, but their efforts were in vain. Desbrisay received three wounds, two in his legs and one on his hand; more seriously hurt was Norbury, who was stabbed twice in the arm and once in the midsection. He died on the spot. Desbrisay was given a trial but there is no evidence that he was punished in any way. An English antidueling law was on the books, but it was largely ignored, and military people were especially immune from prosecution. It also came out that Desbrisay was a drunken, quarrelsome officer and had been reprimanded on several occasions.

One of the most famous early duels took place in 1777 just outside (old) Savannah, in Sir James Wright's pasture, which is close to today's Thunderbolt Road. The combatants were men of prominence who had been mad at each other for some time, Button Gwinnett and Gen. Lachlan McIntosh.

Gwinnett, a signer of the Declaration of Independence, was a leading political figure and had hopes of becoming the first Georgia governor. However, he had made powerful enemies and one of them was General McIntosh, commander of the militia. The two had heaped abuse on each other and Gwinnett was especially bitter when McIntosh referred to him as a "scoundrel and lying rascal." A challenge was issued and a duel scheduled for dawn, May 16, 1777.

When he heard about the hour, McIntosh is supposed to have replied that "he wasn't accustomed to rising so early," but would be there at the appointed time.

Pistols being the chosen weapons, the seconds loaded a pair of them—each with a single ball—and discussed the distance to be set. It was finally decided that the duelists would stand four full strides apart, a distance of only about twelve to fifteen feet! When it was suggested that they begin back-to-back in conventional dueling style, McIntosh demurred. "By no means," said the general. "Let us see what we are about."

At the given signal, two shots rang out.

It's hardly surprising that at this close range both staggered at once. Gwinnett, the more seriously injured, had a bone shattered in his upper leg. McIntosh, shot in the fleshy part of his thigh, demanded to know if his opponent had had enough or would like another shot.

"Yes," answered Gwinnett, "if somebody will help me up."

At this point the seconds stopped the fight. The combatants were brought together to shake hands and then each, with much assistance, was taken to his own home. McIntosh recovered, but Gwinnett, due largely to improper care of his wound, contracted gangrene and died four days later.

In May 1992 there was a dramatic reenactment of this famous duel on the grounds of the Fort Morris Historical Site in Liberty County. Actors, in full costume and wielding authentic flintlock pistols, followed the historical script closely as they went through two performances. Plans call for this to be an annual event.

During the 1850s there was another lurid duel in Savannah. It all started because of an argument over a billiards game at the old Chatham Club (then located in the building at the southwest corner of Bull and Congress streets). Two young men, both prominent in Savannah society, exchanged angry words and then, as things got hotter, one threw a glassful of wine in the other's face.

The insult could not be ignored. The fellow insulted, Stewart Elliott, issued a challenge and it was accepted by his antagonist, Tom Daniell. Accordingly, the two met at a remote spot across the Savannah River. Designated weapons were rifles, not pistols.

It's interesting that Elliott felt some remorse and did not want the duel. He was ready to accept a reasonable apology, but Daniell would not hear of it. He paid no attention to friends who told him over and over that his life was in danger because Elliott was a crack shot.

As the group gathered, a peculiar demonstration took place, an exhibition of marksmanship planned to bring about a peaceful solution. Picking up a large clod of earth, Elliott tied a string around it and told his second to suspend it from the low branch of a nearby tree.

"I will cut the cord with my bullet so Daniell will see what I can do with my weapon," he explained. Then, almost without taking aim, he fired and severed the string.

Daniell's response to this was anger. He was certainly not going to be cowed into submission. "Damn it, he must fight!" was his reaction.

Elliott, perhaps predicting the outcome, still wanted to avoid the confrontation, but there was no alternative. Thus, with seconds and a surgeon standing by, the two stepped off twenty-five paces and took their positions, facing each other with rifles held loosely in hand. Upon command, the two fired almost simultaneously. Daniell fell dead with a bullet through the heart.

The location of this duel was Screven Ferry, just across the Savannah River in South Carolina. At that time there was much antidueling sentiment in the city, so gentlemen, to satisfy their honor, would pick a remote dueling ground. Screven Ferry was a desolate stretch that had been a rice plantation; for a period of seventy years, it was just the spot for pistols at dawn.

Then there was the "three-weapon" duel," a dramatic confrontation between two Camden County men on October 5, 1837. Participants were Charles R. Floyd and Edward Hopkins; location was the beach at Amelia Island.

Here's the scenario: First the opponents were to stand back to back, walk a specified distance, turn at the signal and fire with shotguns. If no one fell, they would advance a set number of paces and switch to horse pistols. Now, if both were still standing, they would again advance and finish off with bowie knives! Hopkins, however, was seriously wounded at the first shotgun blast. This ended the duel.

In 1804, Vice President Aaron Burr killed Alexander Hamilton in a duel. Much public resentment was aroused, and the ill feeling continued to grow. Burr decided he'd have to hide out until things cooled off, so he came to St. Simons Island to visit his old friend, Maj. Pierce Butler, at Hampton Point.

By the end of the nineteenth century laws were toughened and gentlemen began to realize that those old-fashioned codes of honor were not so sacred after all. Dueling became a thing of the past.

TRANSPORTATION MILESTONES

THIRTY-FOUR

THE GREAT TRAIN RACE OF 1901

And the Winner Is . . .

Albert Lodge, engineer on the Plant System freight train from Tampa to Savannah, was a positive fellow. More than that, the small, wiry Lodge was a man of steely determination when a challenge was tossed his way.

The date was March 1, 1901, and Lodge was at the controls of Plant engine Number 111, which had just pulled into Fleming, Georgia, for a water stop. People there seemed awfully excited, he thought, and he soon knew the reason. Another Plant engine, Number 107, had just limped into town after a breakdown on a Savannah to Jacksonville run. But this was no ordinary trip; Number 107 had been in a desperate race with a Seaboard Railways train, staged by the government, with a lucrative U.S. mail contract going to the winner.

There had been plenty of hoots and jeers as the Seaboard train thundered past the stalled Number 107 just south of Savannah; and when her dejected crew brought her slowly into the tiny whistle stop, it didn't appear there was any way they could get back in the race. At that point they saw Lodge come in for water and they rushed over to ask if he'd be willing to switch engines. Lodge, confident of what his machine could do, agreed.

In those days, profitable mail contracts were actively sought by the railroads and were often settled by a speed trial. The winner of this particular race would obtain the mail service to Cuba and the West Indies.

Competing against the Plant System, the railroad arm of empire builder Henry B. Plant, who also had interests in hotel, shipping, and express businesses, was the Seaboard Line, which was making a name for itself along the coastal routes. Seaboard began with a big advantage. Its tracks followed a straight line between the two terminal cities while those of the Plant System made an annoying detour, cutting inland from a point twelve miles out of Savannah to Waycross, then swerving back southeast to Jacksonville, a distance of 149 miles, making its route 31.8 miles longer than the rival line. Engineer Lodge, however, was not a man to let such things bother him. He had a reputation for getting everything possible from an engine and now with an expert hand he coaxed the throttle and soon the driving wheels were churning. It had been almost an hour since the breakdown and every minute counted.

Number 111 (also known as the Rhode Island Lady) pulled four cars, as did the Seaboard locomotive, this having been set by the Post Office Department. Its engine, twin of the crippled Number 107, was a ten-wheeler, with four small front cylinder wheels and six huge driving wheels, six feet in diameter, Highly regarded for its speed and power, it was the same model Casey Jones was piloting on the Illinois Central when he had his famous wreck and hurtled himself into song and legend. Guest riders in the cab with Lodge were S. S. McClellan, a railroad official, and a second engineer and a fireman. Orders were telegraphed ahead: "Clear the track and set and lock all switches."

On the southwest leg to Waycross, the train gathered speed at an alarming rate. Noticing this, McClellan pulled out his timing watch. Over a measured five-mile stretch, he and the second engineer recorded identical times: 2 minutes and 30 seconds, or 120 miles per hour. Incred-

An old steam train similar to the vintage "No. 111," is used for excursion rides in rural Georgia. [Courtesy *Seabreeze Magazine*]

ible but true, they had surpassed the record set in May 1893 of 112.5 miles per hour by the New York Central, an occasion commemorated by a U.S. postage stamp issue.

At Waycross, service crews were ready. A track change took only three minutes and Number 111 was back on its way, now heading southeast on its final leg to Jacksonville. Lodge pulled the throttle wide for straightaways but whenever a curve loomed ahead, the men in the cab were especially concerned. On one of these McClellan, noting the engineer hadn't slowed much, found himself in a heavy sweat wondering if the train would take the turn or "take to the woods." Somehow all curves were negotiated, although the engine lurched madly and the wheel flanges screeched. The coal passer was so terrified on one curve that he flattened himself, face down, on the iron floor.

At Callahan, twenty miles north of Jacksonville, McClellan again checked his watch, and once more for several miles he clocked 120 miles per hour. As they pulled into the Jacksonville terminal, a crowd greeted them with a loud ovation. It was only after they stopped that the men of Number 111 found out they had won; the Seaboard train had not yet arrived. Like the hare racing the tortoise in the fable, their rival, after passing the disabled Number 107, had simply taken their time.

The hero of the great race, Albert Lodge, whose courage and can-do spirit had won the day, accepted the hearty handclasps of his fellow trainmen. The event, ending safely as it did, resulted in much favorable publicity for southern railroads.

A year later the Atlantic Coast Line took over the Plant System. The faithful Number 111, which had broken every existing record for a steam train, remained in service until 1942.

THIRTY-FIVE

THE ALTAMAHA

When Lumber Was King

An old-timer from the logging era wouldn't recognize today's lumber industry in the Peach State.

The slow process of rafting logs down the river was primitive compared to forestry technology that is boosting Georgia to national leadership. The industry contributes more than $12 billion annually to the state's economy, with more than two million tons (hardwoods, softwoods, paper, and allied products) shipped through Georgia ports.

The old raftsman would be amazed that primary wood-using industries process more than three billion board feet of timber yearly, including sawmill output, veneers, and plywood. Nor could he comprehend the scope of the state's pulpwood business in paper manufacture.

Muscle got the logs out of the woods in the old days, with a helpful assist from a team of oxen or horses and a set of "big wheels" to lift them off the ground. Nowadays a tractorlike device called a "skidder" uses a giant mechanical claw to pick up the logs and take them to a waiting truck.

No old-timer could have imagined modern freeways, on which log trailers bearing forty-foot-long cypress logs are a common sight. And he surely would be awestruck to see lumber moved out of the woods by helicopter. Chopper

*When lumber was king in the heyday of the old rafting
era, great rafts of virgin pine logs from the upper Altamaha covered the river at Darien. You could walk from
raft to raft.*

harvesting in Georgia can produce thousands of board
feet a day of cypress, yellow poplar, and blackgum in remote areas where it's the only practical way to get the
timber out.

When lumber emerged as a vital industry in the early
1800s, the state's major rivers were used to float the logs
to market. The Altamaha, comprising 137 miles of wide,
silt-laden water formed by the confluence of the Ocmulgee
and Oconee rivers, handled much of the trade for a long
period and produced a legacy of lore.

Prior to 1819, lumber was cut and moved in a small
way. In that year the first steam sawmill appeared on the
Altamaha. Now a much greater quantity could be mar-
keted, so lumberjacks began cutting more wood and lug-
ging it to the riverbank for a free float ride to the ocean

port of Darien. At this point, however, there was a problem. In other parts of the country logs were dumped into rivers and floated to sawmills in one great mass, often resulting in jams. This was impractical on the Altamaha where there was traffic from steamboats and other craft. Therefore, around 1830, it was decided that the best way to avoid blocking the river would be to use rafts.

Initially, the rafts were crude rectangular affairs, usually thirty-five to forty feet long and fifteen feet wide. The hardwoods closest to the river—cypress, ash, oak, and sweetgum—were the first to be logged, because these could be readily cut and rafted. Green cypress was too heavy to float, so loggers would ring the trees to kill them, then let them dry out for a year before cutting them.

There was no cargo. Raft timbers themselves were the only ones being taken to the mills, and they were easily broken up by obstructions in the river. Also, they were vulnerable to any sort of eddy or "suck" that would pull them into the trees. When that happened, the only way to get them out was to have them pulled back into the cur-

The plans of a post-Civil War pine timber raft called for a fire box, lean-to (goat house), and bow and stern oars that swiveled for ease in steering and propelling the craft forward.

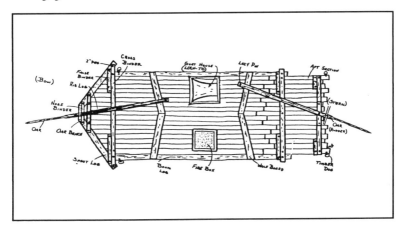

rent by a steamboat. Sometimes there was a wait of a day or two before one came along to do this.

As the rafts approached Darien, they would slow for the wait at the mills and it was said one could walk from raft to raft for a mile or more. Collecting booms above the town extended for about three miles up the river. In the harbor, large cargo vessels loaded the timber, while outside in Doboy and Sapelo sounds, more ships waited (those of foreign registry unable to enter the harbor because of their deep drafts).

At the end of their usefulness, the rafts had to be inspected for value, then dismantled and taken to the saws. Afterwards, the raftsmen would hike back upriver, living on whatever game they could shoot on the way home.

The Altamaha achieved an international reputation. Its lumber, highly rated for quality and durability, was used in the bridge across the Isthmus of Panama, in the Brooklyn drydocks, and in fine homes in Europe.

The Civil War brought a halt to lumber production and Darien itself became a casualty, mostly destroyed by fire. The postwar boom was not long in coming, however. By 1868, the rebuilt town's timber exports topped twenty million board feet and in 1874, some 100 million. Altamaha lumber was again recognized throughout the world and the cargo ships returned. Several foreign governments established consulates in Darien.

Back, too, came the raftsmen, now plying their trade with improved techniques. Postwar rafts had pointed fronts for easier handling and both a bow and stern oar. These were mounted on swivels to help in steering and also to generate forward motion when worked back and forth. The crew consisted of three men, with the most experienced oarsman standing in the front.

There was no cabin, but sometimes a lean-to or tent would shelter the crew. A sandbox enabled the men to build a fire while afloat, and they would cook fatback and corn pone. At sundown, they tied up and camped for the night. A roaring fire was built and the crewmen would

One can get an idea of the size of the Altamaha rafts from this photo, shown with several men aboard.

dine on bacon and sweet potatoes, drinking coffee and swapping stories. Sometimes on quiet nights they could hear other raftsmen talking forty miles downstream, but because of the crookedness of the river, they were only a couple of miles apart.

In the late 1800s, the most sought-after wood was yellow pine. The men would cut during the winter, then in late March take advantage of spring floods to build their rafts and shove off for the mills.

The river held few secrets from the men who rode it day and night, making trip after trip. Legends grew and tall tales got taller with the telling. One pilot, bragging at the evening campfire, would boast that he knew the Altamaha so well that he could tell where he was even on the darkest night just by tasting the water.

There were danger spots, and the raftsmen had to be

constantly on the lookout for snags, which would easily rip a raft apart, as well as for the bights and sucks around each point. Mad Dog Point, Box Point, and Old Hell Bight were noteworthy. Then there was Old Woman's Pocket, a place where an old woman once was asked how deep it was and she replied, "Came up to my pocket." Apparently Old Devil's Shot Bag was named after an old man (old devil) crossed the river.

Farther downstream was Rag Point, a thick growth of bushes projecting into the stream. In the old days, articles of clothing hung in profusion on the limbs of these bushes: breeches, coats, caps, jackets, drawers, socks, shirts, and even women's attire such as petticoats. The story goes that a tenderfoot, making his first trip, was told to hang a piece of clothing there or suffer the consequences: either a dunking or a docking. Dunking was an unfriendly dip in the river and docking meant he'd be docked for the drinks in Darien.

The peak year for Altamaha lumber was 1900 when more than twelve million board feet were officially measured and sold. By World War I, the boom times were over, although rafts occasionally made their way downriver as late as the 1920s and the early 1930s.

The decline started when the forests were being depleted and trains were carrying more and more of the lumber. It took a raft three weeks to haul what a train could handle in one day. As the rafts dwindled, Darien found itself bypassed by the major rail lines. This, combined with the shallowness of its harbor, brought the town down from its former eminence.

But if Darien was down, other towns were springing up. Lumber became the chief export of Jesup, Ludowici, Mount Pleasant, and Sterling Station. Some timber was carried by steamboat after the raft era but highway transportation put the river traffic out of business for good in the 1930s.

Commerce and profits, however, are not the only factors making Georgia's future in forest products bright. Recent advances in paper research and technology could establish the state's dominance in the field.

The relocation of the Institute of Paper Chemistry (now the Institute of Paper Science and Technology) from Appleton, Wisconsin, to Georgia Tech gave the state tremendous status as a research center. Also helping is the expansion and modernization of the Herty Foundation in Savannah that conducts pilot tests under contract for the paper industry. Truly, Georgia is becoming a world center for pulp and paper research and production, with more than thirty paper corporations, dozens of allied suppliers, and millions of acres of forest land.

THIRTY-SIX

INDIAN INGENUITY

Days of the Dugouts

The early East Coast Indians used dugout canoes, and when the colonists first saw them they laughed, saying they looked like hog troughs because the ends were left blunt.

Yet the settlers liked them, and persuaded the Indians to make dugouts for them.

To Native Americans, dugouts were an important means of transportation. Cut from a single log, they were hollowed out by controlled burning and subsequent chopping and scraping. Later, in the hands of the colonists, a more sophisticated craft appeared with a rounded front end. By the nineteenth century, dugouts became sharply pointed, often at both ends.

In Georgia the preferred mode of travel for most planters was a large dugout hewn from a sizable cypress log. During the cotton prosperity of the 1800s they were a common sight on the streams and bayous bordering the plantations.

These dugouts would be up to forty feet long, rowed by six, eight, ten, or even twelve slaves, each holding one oar. These "watermen" were not only adept at handling the boats but also had the stamina for a long haul. They would sing as they stroked, alternating traditional spirituals such as "Roll, Jordan, Roll" and "When I Come to Die" with improvised boating songs.

With all this water activity, racing was sure to become "the thing." Dugouts traveling in company or meeting each other had ample opportunity for a speed test, and the story goes that when this happened crews would peel off their jackets and encourage each other, while the boats fairly leaped ahead. Afterwards, winning crewmen would exult over their victory and crow over the vanquished.

The first strictly racing canoe was a thirty-four-footer, wedge-shaped at bow and stern, and narrow (less than three feet at the widest point). Owned by John Floyd, a Camden County planter (see Chapter 23), this craft would regularly beat the competition in spite of its one drawback: being highly unstable, or tippy.

By the 1830s, racing was an organized coastal sport.

During the 1930s, two old-style plantation dugouts were built at Darien and raced in exhibitions, under six oars. [Courtesy of Sea Island Company]

Competitive dugouts were built, not for comfort, but for speed, being less than thirty-five feet long and with no more than eight oars. A coxswain, usually the plantation owner, would sit in the stern and steer. There would be advance publicity, followed by plenty of excitement, and a big crowd would gather on the bank as race time neared. The race course was a straight mile of river.

Naturally there had to be wagers for the favorites. Bets at one 1838 race included a cigar, a glass of toddy, a pair of boots, and some cash. Not to be outdone, the slave crews would make their own bets, such as a chew of tobacco or some such item.

Race day was a colorful affair. When the Floyds came to St. Simons in 1834, they brought five of their boats and swept the field. One contest pitted their *Goddess of Liberty*, a blue and white craft displaying twenty-four stars, against T. F. Bryan's *Columbia*. Both were six-oared dugouts. *Goddess* won by thirty seconds, to the deafening roars of her cheering section.

Next came a fascinating race between two Floyd boats, the *Goddess* and the *Devil's Darning Needle*, an evil-looking sliver of black. It ended in a perfect tie.

Owners added to the ambience of race day by costuming their watermen for showmanship. For a major race one crew was dressed all in white with red kerchiefs; their rivals, also in white, sported blue turbans. Crewmen never arrived at the course via their own power. They would be towed to save their strength, and one account says they might be hauled as much as eighty miles.

Coastal Georgia's well-known Couper family entered many of their boats in the annual regattas. James Hamilton Couper liked to design racers and in 1852 came up with the *Becky Sharp*, a forty-three-footer with a thirty-three-inch beam. In the regatta at Charleston that year, she won against stiff competition, making ten miles per hour. "Not a false stroke was made," Couper noted. "She rode the water like a duck, with a continuous gliding motion."

In 1837 planters were confident enough to issue a challenge to the New York boat clubs. They suggested a contest against "any four-oared Northern plank boat" to determine whether a dugout was superior.

For a time, the challenge aroused only lofty silence from the Yankee boating brethren. Finally a race was arranged between the *Star,* a Northern clinker-type boat, and a dugout named the *Lizard.* The face-off took place at Savannah in 1838 and the dugout won.

During those antebellum years the planters were prosperous and the spirit of the times was embodied in the races along the rivers, with the cheering crowds, the wagering, the happy fun of sporting life. It was a lifestyle that was not to last. It came to an end with the Civil War.

THIRTY-SEVEN

FLOATING LUXURY

The Yachts of Jekyll

The Englishman was a guest on Vincent Astor's 263-foot *Nourmahal*. He was a rather fussy sort, quick to notice things that were "not quite right."

Therefore when he looked into the crew's mess, he was shocked to see crewmen eating not on the bare table but with classy tablecloths under their plates.

"Sailors with tablecloths," he gasped. "What would Lord Nelson have to say?"

Astor was only one of the millionaires who arrived in style at the Jekyll Island Club in the heyday of the famous resort. His *Nourmahal* wasn't as big as some, but it was very luxurious. On it, he loved to host dignitaries and his most famous guest, who fished with him, was President Franklin D. Roosevelt.

Coming south for the season, January through March, some of the well-heeled club members would arrive in Brunswick in fancy, private railroad cars. Others preferred to cruise the island on their own "bauble of the deep" and felt miffed if someone else had a longer yacht.

None of the Jekyll yachtsmen was more showy than John Pierpont Morgan with his *Corsair*. Four ships of this name were owned by the Morgan family, each mightier than the last. It was the elder Morgan who supposedly

Corsair IV was the largest of the Morgan yachts, at 343 feet. Too big for the Jekyll dock, she had to anchor out in the channel. [Courtesy Jekyll Island Museum]

said that if one had to ask the cost of a yacht he had no business owning one.

And certainly money was no object for J. P. Morgan. *Corsair* I, built in 1881, was a measly 165 feet. When the scowling tycoon noted rivals with longer boats, he ordered his second *Corsair*, a 241-footer, in 1891. The "I've-got-a-bigger-yacht-than-you-have" race was on. Somewhat later, in 1899, J. P. ordered *Corsair* III, which measured 304 feet.

It remained for Morgan's son Jack to top it off with *Corsair* IV, at 343 feet, launched in 1930. This vessel lasted through the Depression, making occasional trips to the island in the late thirties, then it was taken over by the navy in World War II. After the war she became a cruise liner. Both III and IV were too big for the landing dock and had to anchor far out in the channel.

When the Morgan party arrived it was grandeur in the

extreme. As the craft approached, a cannon would be fired on the clubhouse lawn and immediately a bunch of servants would shove off in small boats. As the great mogul was rowed in, a line-up of attendants, uniformed and wearing white gloves, would stand at attention. When all was just right, the imperial Morgan would step ashore.

Joseph Pulitzer, the famous publisher, was a Jekyll yacht-owner. He liked to escape the hectic newspaper business by coming to the island on his 250-foot *Liberty*. Almost blind, Pulitzer ordered his yacht built with no sharp projections in the passenger compartments. It had to be soundproofed to guard him from excess noise. Nevertheless, he enjoyed his music room and gymnasium and kept in touch with his office by telegraph. Pulitzer died on his ship in 1911 in Charleston harbor.

Other Jekyllites in the yachting set included Pierre Lorillard with the *Caimen;* William K. Vanderbilt, *Alva* and *Valiant;* George F. Baker, *Viking;* E. T. Stotesbury, *Castle;* Richard T. Crane, *Illyria;* and Theodore N. Vail, *Speedwell* and *Northwind.*

Magnates with floating palaces who were not Jekyll Island Club members often visited. Among these annual visitors were Ernest B. Dane aboard his *Vanda;* Hiram Manville, the asbestos king, who owned the *Hi Esmaro;* and E. H. Johnson, president of the Victor Talking Machine Company, on his 279-foot *Caroline.*

By World War II the club had disbanded and the postwar era saw fewer and fewer of the great luxury vessels. Taxes increased and many of the tycoons found it hard to maintain both an estate and a yacht. They bought smaller status symbols such as cabin cruisers and left ownership of the really big ships to fellows like Aristotle Onassis.

THIRTY-EIGHT

COAST TO COAST

Brunswick Flyer Breaks Record

In this day of jet airliners and space shuttles, how strange it seems to look back at the early days of flight when it was an awesome event just to cross the continent. In 1921 however, an Army aviator from Brunswick amazed the nation with a record-breaking flight from coast to coast.

Lt. William DeVoe Coney belonged to the 91st Aero Squadron, stationed at Sacramento, California. In February 1921 he was authorized by the Army Air Corps (as it was called then) to show, with a daring exhibition flight, just what military airplanes could do; he would criss-cross the country in a solo flight. The young flyer went at the assignment with relish. Coney, 27, was the second pilot chosen for the grueling trip from San Diego to Jacksonville (the first candidate was forced down in Texas).

Coney's plane, a DeHaviland-4, was an undistinguished two-seater biplane, an awkward, lumbering holdover from the First World War. The craft had been dubbed "the flying coffin" because of its clumsiness, and no amount of fixup or rebuilding seemed to do much to improve its flying characteristics.

Apparently such things did not bother Lieutenant Coney as he watched ground crews adding extra fuel tanks and fitting his plane for the long-distance flight.

Lieutenant Coney at the controls of his plane, a
DeHaviland-4 (originally a two-seater, but the forward
cockpit has been covered up). On the side of the fuse-
lage are U.S. Army identification markings. The picture
was taken at Windsor Park in Brunswick, where Coney
had landed after his triumphant flight to Jacksonville.
[Courtesy Coastal Georgia Historical Society]

When he took off from San Diego on February 21, he felt
confident with 274 gallons of gas—enough to make Jacksonville with one refueling stop. He would attempt to
break the existing transcontinental record of 25 hours,
59 minutes, set by Maj. T. C. McCaulay in 1919.

In those days, aircraft were not equipped with radios,
but Coney had two reliable compasses. He set his course
by following railroad tracks and correcting for the wind
and striving to maintain a straight heading.

His route lay across Arizona mountain ranges but he
was prepared for the chills of a high altitude; he wore a
leather flying helmet, gloves, and a heavy overcoat. He
also carried a parachute.

Dallas was a scheduled refueling stop, and the young aviator was nearly there when a sputtering engine gave him a bad scare. Quickly, he landed at Bronte, Texas, and diagnosed the problem as clogged-up fuel lines. He phoned the air service at Love Field in Dallas; within the hour two mechanics flew over with a new carburetor and the means to clean out his tanks and gas lines. This was a time-consuming operation and it was not until the next morning that the airplane was able to resume its flight.

Coney, now with a fully operational machine, made a short hop to Dallas. Most of the afternoon was spent preparing for a takeoff that night. During this time Coney was able to get a few hours of much-needed sleep.

All went well as Coney headed east under clear skies, bucking northerly winds as he passed Shreveport, Louisiana. He climbed to 7,000 feet so he'd have gliding room to avoid the swampy Mississippi delta in case of a forced landing. At 6:30 A.M. on February 24 he saw the smoke of Jacksonville, stark against the glow of a sunrise over the Atlantic.

Sweeping low over the city, Coney decided to "buzz" the Mason Hotel (later named the Mayflower) where his parents were staying; this would let them know he had finished the trip safely. Then he landed at Pablo Beach (now Jacksonville Beach). Word of his flight had gotten out, and a crowd gathered to congratulate him. Admirers followed as he made his way to the army base at Camp Johnson (now the U.S. Naval Air Station) to report his success to his superior officers.

Later that day, Coney attended a luncheon in Jacksonville to welcome another visiting dignitary: President-elect Harding. The flyer sat at Harding's right hand and, as the number two guest of honor, made a short speech.

Coney's trip made national headlines. He completed the record-breaking solo transcontinental flight (some 2,070 miles) in a flying time of 22 hours, 27 minutes.

The young lieutenant returned to his hometown and became the toast of Brunswick. There were parties and dances galore, and the Young Men's Club awarded him a special loving cup.

But Brunswick would soon go into mourning. Tragedy struck only a few weeks later when Coney was killed on March 26, 1921, in a crash landing in Mississippi. While attempting to break his own record on a return trip to the West Coast, he was thrown from the cockpit. A newspaper clipping, says "there was not a dry eye in the town of Brunswick."

THIRTY-NINE

ROLLING DOWN THE RIVER

The Glory of Paddle Wheelers

Riverboat gamblers, the race between the *Natchez* and the *Robert E. Lee,* hoopskirted Magnolia singing aboard the *Show Boat*—all these images evoke romantic times on the Mississippi River.

However, riverboats also plied Georgia streams and steamboats were important means of transportation, carrying freight and passengers along its coast throughout most of the nineteenth century.

Sometimes the paddle wheel would be at the side, sometimes in the rear, but most common on these coastal vessels was the sidewheeler, which could fare equally well in rivers or sheltered ocean waters. Built mostly in the Northeast, these paddlers had one or two decks, fairly luxurious passenger accommodations, and limited freight capacity. They presented a graceful, even stately appearance.

As early as 1840 there was passenger service, linking such cities as Charleston, Savannah, and Jacksonville. Traffic increased in the decade before the Civil War, then during the hostilities many of the riverboats became blockade runners for the Confederacy. The majority of these were destroyed by Yankee guns, but a few returned at the end of the war to resume their passenger runs.

It didn't take long for postwar entrepreneurs to build new steamboats and get them into service. One of the busiest ships on the coastal run was the *Dictator*, making connections between Charleston, Jacksonville, and Palatka, Florida, from 1865 to 1878. In the 1870s she was joined by the *City Point*, and these two made many trips along the coast. "The safest, cheapest, and only comfortable way to Florida," proclaimed one advertisement. "There's a first-class table and clean, comfortable staterooms. Both New York-built steamers—no extra charge for meals and staterooms. All railroad tickets good by this line."

From 1874 to about 1908 St. Simons Mills, at what is now Epworth By the Sea, turned out great quantities of lumber. Among sidewheelers making regular stops there for the cargo were the *Florida, City of Bridgeton*, and the *David Clark*.

The *Henry B. Plant* was a popular sidewheeler on a route approximating today's Intracoastal Waterway. The ship ran between Fernandina and Brunswick, connecting with trains at both points. Later, she cruised the St. Johns River and was destroyed by fire in 1890.

In 1884 the 123-foot *City of Brunswick* (formerly the *Thomas Collyer*) began coastal runs on what was called the Cumberland Route between Brunswick and northern Florida. This was an old sidewheeler, built in 1850 in New York, with a colorful history on the Potomac and James rivers and Chesapeake Bay. She would leave Brunswick each morning at 8:00 a.m., calling at Jekyll, Cumberland, Dungeness, and Fernandina.

In 1897 the Brunswick, then forty-seven years old, was transferred to Jacksonville for daily trips between that city and Mayport, Florida. On one unlucky day, while she was moored to her dock at Mayport, fire, believed caused by spontaneous combustion, broke out in her coal bunker. At the time, all freight and passengers had been unloaded and her captain was alone on board.

The skipper leaped into action. Noting the rapid spread

of the blaze, he ran to the dock, recruited some dock workers, and ordered the mooring lines cut. The tide carried the flaming hulk to a nearby marshy creek and she burned to the water's edge. Ironically, she had been scheduled to go into the yards for maintenance and repairs that very night. At the time of her destruction, the sidewheeler was one of the oldest steamers on active duty in the United States.

The peak years for the riverboats came in the 1880s. After that, there was a slow decline, mostly due to the competition of the railroads. There were a few old paddle wheelers still afloat in the early twentieth century, but generally their day was done.

FORTY

BRUNSWICK
Heritage of a Busy Port

A 1909 brochure proudly describing Brunswick's industrial scene called the Georgia metropolis, "One of the great seaport cities of the South!"

It was true, then, for the city had been growing since the Civil War and was especially proud of its harbor, sufficient for all but the deepest-draft vessels. It is true today, for miles and miles of inland waterways connect with the ample, picturesque harbor, in use since the Creek Indians paddled in and out in their dugout canoes.

Other dugouts appeared in the plantation era after the War of 1812. The long canoes went up and down the coastal rivers as slaves carried masters and guests where they wanted to go and sang as they stroked along.

After the Civil War there were built tremendous railroad terminals for coal, foodstuffs, and other products coming in by rail, to be transferred for shipping to various parts of the world. A huge ice plant provided cooling for ships and railroad cars carrying perishables. A mammoth coal chute cascaded the fuel into ships' bunkers.

Not many know that Brunswick, at the turn of the century, was the leading shipping port for railroad ties worldwide, about three and one-half million pieces yearly. "From the tree to the trade" was the slogan of the American Tie

180

The Colonel's Island terminal at the port of Brunswick is
a large center for the importation of automobiles.
[Courtesy *Seabreeze Magazine*]

and Timber Company. The lumber volume there (ties and other timber products) exceeded any other port on the South Atlantic. Huge four-masted schooners constantly arrived to load lumber for shipment to various global locations.

The Strachan Line was prominent in the shipping business. It furnished steamer freight service and maintained spacious sheds where cotton and other goods were kept under cover.

During World War I the city came into its own as a ship-building center. In 1917–1918 Brunswick Marine Construction Company built five great four-masted vessels, all in the 200-foot class. One of them was the *Sir Thomas Lipton,* named for the celebrated Irish yachtsman and founder of the well-known tea company.

During World War II. Brunswick was a center for the construction of Liberty ships, large, bulky cargo vessels that carried supplies to America's armed forces around the world. They had straight sides and a flat bottom, being more like tubs, someone observed, than ships. However, they performed their function superbly. The first one rolled off the ways in July 1942, after 331 days in construction. By the end of 1944 the yard was turning them out in little more than a month, with the record being thirty-four days.

As a memorial to the homely old Liberty ships, a special civic committee was formed in 1990 to spearhead a drive to place a replica where the public could see it. Today this twenty-two-foot model stands near the causeway entrance to St. Simons Island near the Welcome Center.

In 1986 International Auto Processing Company began bringing in one make of foreign car. Since then imports have increased to include several other makes. Over 92,000 cars were imported and exported in the calendar year 1996; while the total number of ships entering the harbor was 444, handling over two million tons.

From Indian canoes to huge container ships, this Georgia port's operations have been on target, and today, literally, Brunswick's ship has come in!

EPILOGUE

THE LURE CONTINUES

Blackbeard the pirate couldn't have been all wrong. The old cutthroat liked the Georgia coast. After all, it was close to the Spanish Main and was a good place to lie in wait for galleons carrying gold from the New World to Spain. It's rumored that Blackbeard stashed treasure around here, but nobody has ever found it. The old scalawag even had a Golden Isle named for him.

The legendary pirate was only one of many who liked what they found along the coastal inlets. It's not just the scenery of the place; it's the lure, the magic, the "feeling" that exudes from the very ground, not to mention the magnolias, azaleas, and wind-blown, mossy oaks.

Many travel the world over looking for a "perfect" place to retire or spend a vacation. When they find it—temperate climate, flawless scenery—they don't stay there. Prices might be impossible, or maybe the facilities are too primitive, or it's too remote, too lonely.

(This reminds me of the story of the girl who was looking for the perfect fellow. She looked high and low but when she finally found him, she couldn't marry him. He was looking for the perfect woman.)

Perfection is impossible to find, but the Golden Isles seem to have fewer drawbacks, pound for pound, than a lot of other places.

P. J. Hoff, the veteran Chicago weather forecaster, who

retired to the Georgia coast in the early 1970s, once said: "Other people were taking vacation trips all over the world. My vacations were spent seeking possible retirement spots. This took me along the Pacific Coast from Victoria to Tijuana and the Atlantic from Key West to Prince Edward Island."

But when Hoff found the coastal isles he stopped looking. "It was a place time had passed by—unspoiled and pleasantly slowed to a walk. That appealed to a guy who was tired of racing his motor to get from Point A to Point B, only to race back to Point A again, known as 'traveling in the best circles.'"

It's been a long time since the last ice age some 25,000 years ago created the present coastline of Georgia with its unique barrier islands.

Since then they've experienced high tides, low tides, hurricanes, Guale Indians, Spanish missionaries, pirates, slaves, planters, and a host of colonizers and explorers. The old hunting trails have given way to modern freeways and the colonial forts have been replaced by homes, factories, and shopping centers.

Where a log cabin once stood bravely near the shore, a giant paper mill now churns out its commercial products. Where a Spanish mission once proclaimed the gospel to the natives, a modern motel seeks to entice tourists. Across the river where Indian canoes once glided, a giant bridge spans a channel along which mammoth container ships carry automobiles from a faraway country.

But history repeats itself: newcomers continue to be drawn by the lure of the land. The incentives are many: good climate, retirement, golf, the beaches, fishing, and simply the yearning for a quieter, more laid-back style of life.

Perhaps there is room for all. Happily, there are many acres of pristine beaches and forest. Marshlands, impossible to develop, stand guard as they add to the loneliness and seem to block off some of the usable, desirable land that might otherwise be subject to the bulldozers. Most of the barrier islands themselves are still remote, accessible only by boat. Not only is there no causeway, but also no roads once you get there.

Growth is likely to continue, however, in other easy-to-get-to coastal places, not only in resort areas but also on the mainland. Retirees and sun-worshipers come, along with an increasing wave of those who want to get away from the hectic pace of busy metropolitan areas. Following these new arrivals come, inevitably, the profit-minded: merchants, entrepreneurs, and developers.

There's constant talk of more roads, grander high-rises, more billboards, bigger harbors, additional causeways to link the islands with the mainland. It's one thing for a place to be attractive and desirable, to make folks glad they came, but there's also cause for concern. Nature lovers, environmentalists, and old-time residents themselves view the growth with misgivings; There's worry over saving beaches, conserving wild, scenic areas, preserving precious wetlands.

Population growth, with its accompanying boost in businesses, condos, and new homes causes worry among coastal residents. They welcome newcomers but they want to be sure of certain things. Will there be orderly growth, proper zoning, and the preservation of the history and beauty of these acres?

History, the main theme in this book, is a partial answer to the problem. There's a lesson in the history of other vacation and resort areas that were so popular that people flocked to them, only to be smothered by overdevelopment. Then, too, there's the influence of historians and ecologists who work to preserve these special areas. One looks with pride at the trail markers and historical plaques along the Great Southern Coast. Certainly these areas, set aside with such devotion for future generations, can help influence the commercial elements to move ahead with care, caution, and compassion.

It isn't heaven in the Golden Isles, because one still has to search the aisles at Winn Dixie for fresh cucumbers and wait in line at the bank and the post office. But a tangy shot of imperfection adds flavor to the overall stew.

If, by perusing these pages, you go away with a sense of the timelessness of this place, and a feel for how history has been a vital part of it all, then maybe you'll feel a little more of the romance, adventure, and captivation others have felt.

All in favor say "Island"!

BIBLIOGRAPHY

Associated Press Sports Staff. *The Sports Immortals.* 1972. Prentice-Hall, Inc., Englewood Cliffs, NJ.

Bailey, Eloise. 1976. *Camden's Challenge.* Camden (County) Historical Commission.

Bartram, William. 1955. *Travels of William Bartram.* New York: Dover Publications.

Bell, Malcolm, Jr., 1987. *Major Butler's Legacy.* Athens, GA: University of Georgia Press.

Burnett, Gene. 1986, 1988. *Florida's Past.* Vols. I and II. Englewood, FL: Pineapple Press.

Cate, Margaret Davis. 1979. *Our Todays and Yesterdays.* Spartanburg, SC: The Reprint Co.

Cate, Margaret Davis. 1955. *Early Days of Coastal Georgia.* New York: Gallery Press.

Durant and Bettman. 1952. *Pictorial History of American Sports.* A. S. Barnes and Co.

Faris, John. 1924. *The Romance of Forgotten Towns.* New York: Harper Brothers.

Fleetwood, Rusty. 1982. *Tidecraft.* Savannah, GA: Coastal Heritage Society.

Gamble, Thomas. 1974. *Savannah Duels and Duelists.* Spartanburg, SC: The Reprint Co.

Garrison, Webb. 1987. *A Treasury of Georgia Tales.* Nashville, TN: Rutledge Hill Press

Georgia Writers' Project (Savannah Unit). 1940. *Drums and Shadows.* Athens, GA: University of Georgia Press.

Ginn, Edwin. 1989. *The First Hundred Years.* Brunswick, GA: Glover Printing.

Graham, Abbie Fuller. 1976. *Old Mill Days.* St. Simons Island, GA: St. Simons Public Library.

Green, R. Edwin. 1982. *St. Simons Island: A Summary of Its History.* Westmoreland, NY: Arner Publications.

Historical Collections of Georgia. 1855. New York: Pudney and Russell.

Holbrook, Stewart. 1953. *The Age of the Moguls.* Garden City, New York: Doubleday.

Huie, Mildred. 1986. *Kelvin Grove, A Patriarchal Plantation.*

Hurst, Robert. 1974. *This Magic Wilderness.* Waycross-Ware (Counties) Centennial Committee.

Ivers, Larry E. 1974. *British Drums on the Southern Frontier.* Chapel Hill, NC: University of North Carolina Press.

Jones, Bessie (with Bess Lomax Hawes). 1972. *Step It Down.* New York, NY: Harper and Row.

Jones, Charles C. 1878. *Dead Towns of Georgia.* Savannah, GA: Steam Printing House.

Martin, Harold H. 1978. *This Happy Isle.* Sea Island Co.

McCash, William B., and Hall, June. 1989. *The Jekyll Island Club.* Athens, GA: University of Georgia Press.

Mellon, Knox Jr. 1973. Christian Priber's Cherokee Kingdom of Paradise. *Georgia Historical Quarterly* 57.

Murray, Alton J. 1976. *South Georgia Rebels.* St. Marys, GA: Author.

Parrish, Lydia. 1942. *Slave Songs of the Sea Islands.* New York, NY: Creative Age Press.

Rohwer, Jurgen. 1983. *Axis Submarine Successes 1939–1945.* Annapolis, MD: Naval Institute Press.

Sheftall, John. 1977. *Sunbury on the Medway.* Georgia Dept. of Natural Resources, Atlanta, GA.

Stevens, William B., *History of Georgia* (Vol. I), Beehive Press, Savannah (1972). (Originally printed 1847).

Sullivan, Buddy. 1990. *Early Days on the Georgia Tidewater.* McIntosh County Board of Commissioners.

Van DeWater, Fred. 1931. *The Real McCoy.* Garden City, NJ: Doubleday.

Vocell, James T. 1914. *History of Camden County.* Author.

Willoughby, Commander Malcolm F. 1964. *Rum War At Sea*. Treasury Department, U.S. Coast Guard.
Wise, Stephen. 1989. *Lifeline of the Confederacy*. University of South Carolina Press.

SPECIAL REFERENCE SOURCES

Collections of the Georgia Historical Society, Vol. VII, Part III, Savannah, GA (1917).
Current Biography Yearbook (various issues).
Contemporary Authors, Vol. 132.
Georgia Historical Quarterly (various issues).
Dictionary of American Negro Biography. 1982. Edited by Rayford W. Logan and Michael Winston. New York: Norton.
Dictionary of Literary Biography. Vol. 91. Edited by Sam G. Riley, Detroit: Gale Research.

PERIODICALS

American History Illustrated, February 1984
The Brunswick News, Brunswick, GA
The Compass (Mobil International), Fall 1974
The Harbor Sound, Brunswick, GA
The Florida Times Union, Jacksonville, FL
The Savannah Morning News, Savannah, GA
The Jekyll Golden Islander, Jekyll Island, GA

INDEX

Bold face indicates photograph or illustration.